GUARDED BY MYSTERY

GUARDED BY MYSTERY

MEANING IN A POSTMODERN AGE

DAVID WALSH

THE CATHOLIC UNIVERSITY OF AMERICA PRESS

WASHINGTON, D.C.

The paper used in this publication meets the minimum requirements
of American National Standards for Information Science—Permanence of
Paper for Printed Library materials, ANSI Z39.48-1984.

∞

LIBRARY OF CONGRESS
CATALOGING-IN-PUBLICATION DATA

Walsh, David, 1950 –
Guarded by mystery : meaning in a postmodern age / David Walsh.
p.   cm.
1. Sociology, Christian   2. Christianity—Philosophy.   3. Meaning
(Philosophy)—Religious aspects—Christianity   I. Title.
BT738.W3325   1999
291.2—dc21
98-50363
ISBN 0-8132-0945-5 (alk. paper)
ISBN 0-8132-0944-7 (cloth)

Guarded by Mystery: Meaning in a Postmodern Age was composed in
10.5/14.5 Adobe Minion by Generic Compositors, Stamford, New York;
printed on 60-pound Glatfelter and bound by Cushing-Malloy, Inc.,
Ann Arbor, Michigan; and designed and produced by
Kachergis Book Design, Pittsboro, North Carolina.

To David B. and David McC.

CONTENTS

ACKNOWLEDGMENTS

It is a pleasure to record again the faithful friendship of Fr. Brendan Purcell of University College, Dublin, who read through the entire manuscript of this book with his usual generosity and acuity. In addition, I have benefitted from the helpful comments provided by the two readers selected by The Catholic University of America Press, Fr. Jim Schall, S.J., of Georgetown University, and Professor Bill Thompson, of Duquesne University. Financial support was provided by the Earhart Foundation as part of their funding of my larger project on the transparence of the modern world. Copyediting was skillfully provided by Philip G. Holthaus, and the publication process graciously overseen by Susan Needham of The Catholic University of America Press.

GUARDED BY MYSTERY

CHAPTER 1

THE LIGHT OF LONGING

Is this all? Is there not something more to life? What am I missing? Surely there must be something more than the daily routine and the fleeting unsatisfactory satisfactions we attain? How can it be that death is the end of it? Life, someone said, is what happens to you when you are planning for something else. In many respects our whole lives seem to be one long preparation for something else. But what? None of us is going to get out of here alive. So what is it that draws us, that constantly beckons us, that absolutely will not let us live in the here-and-now? As far back as the first human traces we have been able to discover, we find evidence of men and women living beyond their immediate circumstances. When we begin to raise such questions explicitly we engage in philosophy.

This book is an attempt to shed what light I have been able to discover on questions that are at the core of every human existence. They are moving increasingly to the center of attention as more of us get older. Life and its sufferings and limits compel us to confront who we are. There is no longer a future of unlimited possibilities, a playground of the imagination, stretching out before us. Advertisers will continue to ply us with the promise of escaping the grinding toll of life, but their products do not work that way. We only purchase a car or obtain a new gadget; we do not buy happiness or bliss. The door that opens up that other endless wonderful realm beyond remains closed to us. Yet we continue to know it is there; otherwise, what would be the appeal of the new? No one could ever sell us anything if it promised only to provide us with more of the same.

Our experience is indeed structured by this living toward another dimension. It is what provides the whole relish for or zest of life. Depression is what overwhelms us when the possibility of attaining that mysterious beyond seems to have almost closed off. We literally feel we have nothing for which to live. This feeling can drive people to suicide because life for them becomes impossible. We seem to be compelled to live for something beyond what we are or have now, and to be driven to believe that it will be qualitatively greater than what we have known up to this moment. We know of course that this belief is an illusion: the future will be similar to the past and no satisfaction will make us finally happy. Our very sanity seems to depend on keeping a balance between our expectations and reality, not veering too far in one direction or another. Leaning too much toward illusion sets us up for disappointment, yet we must continue to anticipate excitement in life. Human beings seem destined to look toward the future as if it were the eternal.

Is it not strange the way even very old people continue to make plans and look forward to what they are going to do, although from our point of view there seems to be so little time left to them? And yet they know this too, that it is all an illusion, that they are chasing a will-o'-the-wisp. What is it that keeps them going, that prevents them from giving up or railing against the emptiness of it all? What is the source of their equilibrium or serenity? Could it be that they have found the balance in seeing that they must continue to play the game while knowing it is only a game? But what, then, enables them to accept this game of chasing shadow happiness? Can it be that they have understood how the shadows play the role of drawing us on to the reality that lies beyond? We are invited into the game by the excitement and mystery it promises, but are drawn ever deeper into utterly unsuspected dimensions.

When we say that all human beings believe in immortality we mean that they all live, of necessity, as if there is an order beyond this life. There is always the horizon of the "something more" surrounding and embracing all that we are and have done. We are not simply the sum of our parts or of our days. We sense that there is more at stake in our actions than mere profit or loss. What we do touches another realm, a realm more serious, more enduring than our petty pains and pleasures. It is because we are in contact with that other realm that we deserve to be taken seriously, not dismissed as one more grubby animal scratching out its existence on the surface of the planet. We are moral beings in the sense that we are aware of a dimension of good and evil beyond the limits of our own egos, that small world of our own feelings and calculations. Whether we like it or not, whether we cooperate with or resist it, we are part of an order that transcends our finite selves and we suspect that that is the most important part of ourselves.

Dostoevsky, in his story "The Dream of a Ridiculous Man," describes a man who has so withdrawn into himself that he has left himself no apparent option except suicide. He is on his way home, resolved to sit down and shoot himself, when a small girl crying in the street tugs at his sleeve. At first the man brushes her off and attempts to go on his way, but the girl stubbornly clings to his clothes. Eventually the man gives in and bends down to talk to her. He consoles her and gives her some help; finally, she is comforted and he is able to get away from her. He makes his way into his house, still resolved to kill himself. He sits down at the table, takes out his revolver, and prepares to shoot himself ... but he cannot. That little girl had broken into his closed consciousness in such a way that now he cannot simply turn his back on reality. The story goes on to recount the dream of human brotherhood the "ridiculous man" has, but none of it would have been possible without the little girl. She is the one who drew him out of himself, put him in contact with the common humanity they share, and showed him that this is a reality far beyond his own petty self-absorption.

All the great experiences of human life have to do with such similar moments of being taken out of ourselves. We "lose ourselves," as people say, but in another sense we "find ourselves" in a deeper level of reality. We are most truly ourselves when we live most fully beyond ourselves. This is why the experience of love, of falling in love and of being in love, is so central in human life. It is no accident that it is the subject of an endless number of novels, poems, stories, songs, operas, and films, because it is a subject of endless fascination to us. In the same way, the birth and subsequent care for our children exercises an almost equal impact on us, drawing us out of ourselves to attend continuously to them and their needs. The other passions that we have, whether they are for sports, politics, art, or music, have some of that same quality. We are drawn into them not because they provide any material return, but because they put us in touch with a level of reality beyond the confines of our own self-enclosed egos.

These events structure our lives, not the days and months and years through which we pass. They are what enable us to get through the mundane, the everyday in which we must continue to perform the daily routine. But it must always be a routine that adds up to more than the sum of the days, and it is sustainable only because we sense a larger reality within and beyond it. There is, for example, nothing exalted about responding to the needs of a sick child or putting up with an irritable husband or wife, but we sense that unless we can somehow stick with it that we will not be able to reach anything of value in our lives. We will have failed to go beyond ourselves when it counted most. In this way we are stretched by life itself beyond what we had ever anticipated. Ordinary human beings are drawn through the ordinary process of life and its responsibilities to become extraordinary. The expansion of our self takes place, sometimes joyfully and sometimes painfully, as we learn the meaning of love.

It is then that the unsuspected depths of life are encountered. We learn that the horizon of mystery surrounding us, with which we seemed to be familiar, could draw us into deeper levels than we had ever known. This is the path of saintliness, of the loss of self that is the true recovery of self. It is the path that is hungered for in the profusion of contemporary spiritualities yet is missed because we cannot believe it includes the horror of the cross. But whether it is recognized or not, it is the only path to illumination. It is there that the real miracle occurs as we encounter the divine presence that is already there waiting to receive us. We recognize him as the silent source of the invitation, the constant companion from the start. The soul that has been tried is consoled and bathed in a love that far transcends anything it has known before. Yet it recognizes that love as familiar, as the reality that was present in all the earlier forms. Now the impossible becomes possible, even easy. The endurance, fidelity, and responsibility that had seemed so heroic before become an inevitable movement of assent now. The limit of what can be known by a human being is glimpsed in that moment.

It is in just such a moment of recognition that we sense the measure by which our lives are to be guided. Nothing has changed for us in the outward reality. We have not acquired any new information, nor have we been let in on some great secret unknown to ourselves or others previously. Everything is as it was, and yet everything is different. It is as if the world goes on as before, while inwardly we have passed into another realm. But that is not true either, since we are who we were beforehand and we have not become any smarter, richer, or stronger. The change is more a change of perspective by which we see the world differently. Contact with that other reality that is ever on the border of our consciousness has jolted us into a recognition of the real proportion of all things. The Greeks referred to this proportion as the "unseen measure" and understood the search for order in individual and political life as a function of the art of measurement. But that brings us no closer to explaining or identifying what goes on in that limiting experience of touching the highest reality, however it may be conceived. The failure of all descriptions is perhaps best captured by the formula used in Exodus to signify the covenant between God and the elders of Israel. It simply says that they went up the mountain where "they beheld God, and ate and drank" (Exodus 24.11). The event in which everything is changed cannot be explained because it is not a change of any specific aspects.

What has changed is the scale by which they are to be viewed. Now we see the frailties and foibles of our life in their true proportion, now we have gained a sense of what is enduring beyond all else. In relation to that greater reality the difficulties and the achievements of our life shrink to their real significance. We sense them as no longer the most important reality, and in the process we have gained a measure of detachment. It is a process that Solzhenitsyn recounts beautifully in the *Gulag Archipelago* as the process by which the prisoners gradually learned to shed the things that held them fast to the cares and concerns of life. At each successive stage of the meditation, Solzhenitsyn intoned the refrain "we are ascending." Now the true prisoners became all of those whose lives are stuck fast in their endless involvement with events, schemes, conflicts, and struggles that promise them only the fleeting satisfaction of still greater difficulty. The actual prisoners had learned to lose everything, to surrender even the care of their own selves to that greater reality beyond and, in the process, had become free. Again externally nothing had changed.

Truth Disclosed in Living Out

But how do we know that this was not an escape? After all, what can be more plausible than that human beings will seek to escape the sufferings of life in the dream of their own chosenness? That is an important question because in the area of spiritual experience we must be constantly on guard against deception and self-deception. Charlatanism can be present even in the places where we least suspect it: *our own hearts*. But perhaps the thing to notice first is this very self-critical suspicion itself. It arises from the desire not to be deceived or deluded and reveals the quest for truth as its own source. Moreover, it reveals the quest as already structured in a preliminary way by a kind of knowledge from the beginning. For the question of separating the bogus from the genuine presupposes that we know or are capable of recognizing the difference between them. We will be able to distinguish the contrived from the real because we know what it is of which we are in search. It is already present as the source of the search itself.

This is also what makes its communication possible. The experiences of being touched by transcendent reality, the unmistakable encounter with a level of reality beyond everything else in our experience, is not a merely private or idiosyncratic experience. While some people seem to have more of an affinity for spiritual experience than most of us and a very few are mystics, none are utterly untouched by the awareness. We are capable of recognizing what the mystics refer to because our own experience is also structured by a horizon of mystery. We recognize ourselves in their accounts. They ring true for us. This is not because we have had the same experiences or because we are capable of reaching the mystical depths, but because we have asked ourselves the same questions from which the experience unfolds. We live toward a level of reality that is beyond the everyday routine, the plodding accumulation of cause and effect that makes up our daily lives. We are appalled by the prospect that there is nothing more than the sum of our days and minutes, that our relationships could be reduced to their crass exchange value. Everything in our lives cries out to be taken more seriously, and we invest the defining life events of births, marriages, and deaths with a sanctity that transcends their factual reality. We recognize the mysterious contact with transcendent being because it evokes the same recognition in ourselves. We know it because in some sense we have already been there.

It is because we all have the same fundamental experience of the human condition that we can communicate and live in a common world. We recognize one another as human beings not merely through physical appearance, but more deeply as sharers in the common experience of wonder at the horizon of mystery we do not comprehend. This is the unfathomable dimension of the person whom we recognize as engaged in the same unending quest for reality as ourselves. We are brothers and sisters because we have come from a common source and are moved toward a common goal by the horizon of transcendent mystery from which we live. The equal dignity of human beings is derived from this sense that we are each touched by an infinity, an inexhaustibility, that can never be fully articulated no matter how long or comprehensive our description becomes. The mystery of the person escapes the tools of our analysis. Only laughter reminds us of the impossibility of capturing in the net of science that which is itself the source of science. Love consists in this, the German poet Rilke observed, that two solitudes bound and guard and greet each other. That is all the instruction we have for building our lives together, but in itself that is enough.

There is no moral blueprint, a set of instructions that comes with a human being detailing how he or she should perform. That might be a good deal less confusing. We might often wish that life were simpler, as people hanker for a vanished past of alleged moral certainties. Instead, it seems to be our destiny to have to find our way. We are free, and freedom requires that the instructions not be built in. They must be discovered, and in the discovery they can be freely chosen or rejected. Indeed, the very process of discovery is embedded in our freedom, so that we will tend not to discover those guidelines that we are less inclined to follow out. Yet even the moral directions that we choose to firmly reject do not quite go away. They are never quite successfully repressed. They remain in the background as the disturbing undertow of a movement or an invitation we have failed to take up. Even when we reject them, they do not go away. We do not invent our own moral order; we do not create our own values. Our freedom is not absolute. It is structured by the same mysterious pull toward a horizon of transcendent reality that we sense as the most important intimation of our lives.

We sense that the moral direction is not merely one option among others, just as we might choose to play golf or to read a book. No, it is the direction that if we were to miss it undermines the value of everything else we do. To fail to live toward it is to fail to live in contact with the only ultimate source of meaning and reality in our lives. We will not only have made the wrong choice, we will have botched our lives. What makes the demands of the moral order so imperious, demands that we cannot afford to ignore, is that they come before us as intimations of the transcendent reality toward which we are drawn. This is why the mystery of existence, no matter how disturbing or incomprehensible it becomes, is all supportable once we know that we are following the direction that leads toward what is worthwhile. It is that attraction that is both the source of our movement toward what is right and the principal source of illumination we have in our struggle. We may not have a complete set of instructions beforehand, but we do gain more and more insight into the process as we follow it out. The movement toward the good that is alone the way worth living reveals itself ever more solidly to us as we yield to its intimations within us. As human beings we are always on the way, we are never finished products. What we are to be and how we are to achieve it becomes clear only to the extent that we seek to follow the most real promptings within us.

This may be unsatisfactory from the point of view of certainty and predictability. It would certainly be more convenient if we could reduce the process of moral development to a formula or a technique. Even a well-defined set of guidelines would be enormously helpful in deciding where right and wrong lie. But there is no schema that can relieve us of the burden of struggling toward the good. Even the Ten Commandments provide no more than general rules; they tell us nothing about how they are to be applied. It is the concrete struggle for moral truth in action that is the whole challenge for us as human beings. Everyone knows that killing is wrong; it is deciding what specific actions count as killing that is the difficult task. Moral norms are more properly understood as abbreviations for a whole set of intimations that are in turn rooted in a broad experience of the order of things. It is this prior level of character and inner orientation that is the crucial level, but how we are to become the kind of good person who sees what should be done in each situation is not so clear. It is absorbed by the circular knowledge that we will know what to become only by living it, and we will live it only by becoming it.

Yet it is not a closed circle because we already find ourselves within it. We would not even have the questions that point us toward good and evil if we did not already experience such intimations within us. The sifting of the moral and the immoral, the virtuous and the vicious is not something that we must undertake without previous acquaintance. No matter where we begin the reflection, no matter how elementary the level, we already begin with the preexisting intimations of the good and the bad within ourselves. Moral development consists of an enlarging and refinement of those intuitions; it does not in any sense replace or create them. Nor can we get back behind such moral intimations to find some deeper level of reality from which they are derived. There is no underlying layer of our experience, whether instinct or self-interest or power, to which they can be reduced. This is because suspicion of the purity of our own motives, the searching examination of our inner intentions, is itself derived from the sense of what is good beyond all calculation and self-concern. Even the scrutiny of our motives as hollow presupposes a sense of what they ought to be. We cannot get beyond the sense of good and evil.

No Escape from Responsibility

The perennial temptation has been, of course, to find some neutral other reality on which to project this existential struggle. It would certainly make human life a good deal less complicated for all of us if it could be reduced to economics or sex or power. The burden of struggling between fidelity and infidelity to a code that discloses itself only so far as we respond to it could be relieved. What could be more pleasant than to be able to surrender the tension of responsibility for ourselves to some other power? But it would also be the end of our humanity. How terrible the prospect of perfection, of ease, and of life without struggle. The question What would we live for? raises its familiar head. For we sense the contraction of horizons as the determination of who we are approaches the level of a problem to be settled. The nightmare quality, the sense of a world closing in on us like the collapse of gravity in a black hole around a dying star, is a crushing weight that overwhelms us. What looked like the release from burden suddenly becomes the most crushing weight imaginable. Endless fulfillment without aspiration would be the end of our humanity. No, we are not made to attain a paradise within time. Give us back the untidy and unruly struggle between good and evil within us.

Let us instead seek to live as human beings, recognizing more fully what that dignity entails. It is not to become the total masters of our fate. Rather, it is to respond to the pull of that which is beyond ourselves, the good that transcends us in a reality we sense as divine, but toward which we have been given the gift of struggling that is alone the means of sharing transcendent life. Freedom is the privilege of a being that cannot be confined to this world. It can only be exercised by rejecting the impulse to dominate the conditions of existence. Freedom cannot be used to escape freedom itself. It cannot be used in a final way to escape the burden of struggle in freedom by attaining the endless peace of enslavement. There is no freedom except in the struggle to attune our lives in accordance with an order we glimpse as utterly beyond us. Once we have asserted our own superiority to the moral order, there ceases to be any need for struggle and therefore for freedom.

If we reach the point where we can assert that we know what man is and that we have solved the riddle of good and evil, then human freedom is finished. This is the mystery that goes all the way back to the Garden of Eden where the temptation is to become like gods by knowing good and evil. When Adam and Eve yielded to that aspiration, as we would all like to step outside the mystery of human existence and take charge of it for ourselves, they reached not divinity but the loss of the paradise they enjoyed. Man cannot pole-vault out of his humanity into the viewpoint of God. The attempt to do so does not result in any great illumination. Rather, it ends in the emptiness of a world deprived of all transcendence, of all sense of a beyond that alone gives human life its tang and excitement. It is the loss of the only paradise available to us and the collapse of human life to the deadness of the mechanical, the finite, and the futile. Paradise remains, but our participation in it depends on our ability to withstand the temptation to bring it under our control and draw it wholly into our earthly existence.

In many respects that fatal mistake has been the source of the confusion and misery of the modern world. We have committed the oldest sin in the book, the sin of human overreaching that attempts to put itself in the place of God. The great revolutionary movements from the eighteenth century up to the present have been driven by the dream of creating a lasting order of justice within this world. They went beyond calling for merely political change to promise universal human emancipation. Liberation from the burden and drudgery of existence was the banner that inspired mass enthusiasm. We were to hurl ourselves into the creation of a new world order, as remnants of that rhetoric still remind us, although no one stopped to reflect that men are incapable of truly *creating* anything, let alone a whole world. We are parts of a world that was created for us and is given to us. We can move within that world and take responsibility for its development, but we cannot step outside of the whole to engage in the activity of creating the world. Our unsuitability for the task and our rootedness within a world is brought home to us in the reflection on the emptiness of the achievement of a perfect world order even if it were possible. It would spell the end of our humanity and the ultimate nightmare of a closed existence.

John Stuart Mill, the great British social reformer of the nineteenth century, is one of the rare few who discovered the truth of this realization in his own experience. After working for decades on schemes for social improvement and political liberalization, as he explains in his *Autobiography*, he woke up one morning to ask himself a simple question: If all that I have been struggling to bring about for all these years were suddenly to come true and my dream of a social transformation were to be realized, would I be happy? To his astonishment, he found that the answer that welled up spontaneously within him was No! His work had all been structured by the presupposition that it could never finally be completed. All of the zest and interest that it held for him as a human being arose out of the security that it was surrounded by a horizon of mystery that constantly beckoned him but could never be surpassed. Mill fell into a depression that lasted for several years as a result of this flash of recognition. Gradually he came out of his dejection, as any other human being might, when he came to realize that, for all of his conviction that he was working to abolish the mystery of transcendence in human life, he had not in fact done so and that there was little danger of such success.

Man Is More than Technique

Mill's reassuring experience is instructive for the broader historical context in the technological dominance of our own society. We very often have the sense of technology as an utterly overwhelming force that dwarfs our capacity to control it. Technology is frequently viewed as the genie we originally let out of the bottle in order to do our bidding, but which turns on us and paradoxically forces us to conform to the same requirement of instrumental efficiency that is the secret of its power. We become victims of the very power we had thought would make our mastery supreme. Just as the clock, a means of measuring and dividing and using time, gave us control over time, so it in turn became a power standing over and determining the way we must live. In order to use time, we must conform to time. To a certain extent this is true. Technology requires our submission to its mechanical discipline if we are to make use of it. But human life continues to escape its final reach. We are incapable of being wholly governed by the instrumentality of technique. It may often appear to us that much of our lives are spent under its tyranny. But it is impossible for it to extend its reach completely and the most centrally human aspects escape it entirely. Just as with the clock, our lives are not really lived within its time. We live in human time where duration is measured by the nature and quality of our experience. Time flies when we are having fun and it drags when we are bored with what we are doing, just as it always has. The time in which we actually live escapes the measurement of the clock.

In the same way, the apparently omnivorous reach of technology reaches its limit in the impossibility of supplying human happiness. There is certainly the promise of fulfilling all of our needs in the development of technological control. And the success of technology within its specified limits is certainly impressive enough to suggest that it might eventually supply all of our wants and wishes. It possesses the undeniable allure of freeing us from a life of struggle. We are no longer living, as Plato suggests in the *Symposium*, between poverty and fullness; the resourcefulness of technology holds out to us a future of ease and satisfaction. But the more we approach it, the further the horizon recedes before us. The distance between technology and the attainment of its goal is preserved. In that disappointment lies our salvation. It is what saves our humanity and establishes the superiority of man over his instruments. The source of all that creativity cannot be absorbed into its own machines. What preserves us from this fate is that as technology enlarges the horizon of our action, the horizon of our aspirations extends even further. Paradoxically, the freedom of human beings is guaranteed by our incapacity to ever attain our fulfillment. It is this that establishes the distance in which technology is seen to be a tool of human beings who far outdistance it in reality and extension.

We can of course succumb to the imperatives of technology and resign ourselves to its rule over our lives. That is always a danger. We can allow ourselves to be mastered by our own machines if we believe that they are capable of fulfilling all our aspirations. But we know that they cannot, and that is the perspective from which we can maintain our control over them. Once they are viewed as making very limited contributions to our happiness, a happiness that will never be complete within any finite limits, technology loses its alien character as a power standing over us. Then with unclouded eyes we see all technological development for what it is: a partial instrument for finite satisfactions of human beings. This is the vantage point from which it must be judged. Since technology does not help us to achieve our ultimate happiness, and never will, we must weigh its value at each stage in relation to our ultimate fulfillment. How compelling is the case for any new technique that will only contribute such a limited improvement to our human condition? Even more, how much support should we give to such a limited technological advance when it threatens to undermine the very core of our humanity? Technology must never be permitted to jeopardize the limitless human reality that is its source.

The challenge we face today is the recovery of that core sense of what our humanity is. After several centuries in which the idea of the distinctively human has taken a beating, we are now at the point where we can begin to think about these issues from a different perspective. Our sense of historical progress is jaded, largely because we have been able to witness so much of it and to recognize that it brings much misery as well as significant achievements. At any rate, it is no longer conceived as a great impersonal force looming over us. Rather, it has shrunk to the modest proportions of our realization that progress is largely confined to the tools at our disposal. Neither we nor the world as a whole have been transformed. We can shed the apocalyptic expectations of a future age of unlimited perfection both in its optimistic and pessimistic variants. Our history has arrived at the point where we can begin to see more clearly what human beings are. To the extent that we are the source of all technology, then there is always a distance between us and what we create. We cannot be included within its frame of reference because we recognize the limits of its application. Nowhere is this distance more evident than in our capacity to worry that we might be absorbed into the logic of the machine.

Concern about the growth of "artificial intelligence" is perhaps the best indication of the extent to which human beings are superior to machines. Charles Darwin had earlier speculated that our convictions about evolution might not be any more reliable than the convictions of monkeys, without noticing that such a question is precisely what indicates our distinctiveness and the source of our capacity for truth. We may not be as strong as the machines we build nor as rapid at manipulating data, but we are capable of maintaining a detachment from all that we do. That is what makes us different from the wholly immediate reality of things. We can ask the question about the meaning of artificial intelligence and wonder how close this brings the machine to the human level. We are aware of the distance that separates us from any of the tasks on which we are engaged. There is a gulf between us and all that we are and do. We are defined, as Aristotle suggested, by our capacity for wonder. We ask questions about what is not present. We are never wholly absorbed into the task, the purpose, the project. Nor are we ever wholly satisfied with the result. Perfection is unknown to us and even satisfaction is evanescent. Everything about us proclaims our trajectory beyond this world. We are the highest reality *within* it, and consequently its undisputed master, because we are never wholly *of* it. Our dominion is ultimately derived from our vantage point outside of all space and time.

Yet we are not the supreme masters of reality. Our own mastery is derived from our relationship to that which is truly the source of all things. In itself our capacity to transcend all situations and satisfactions is an empty restlessness. It points us toward the futile search for meaning and fulfillment within this world. Only a transcendent reality can be the adequate goal of our searching and striving. Indeed, we would hardly even have this unlimited reach of thought and aspiration if we did not already carry within us the awareness of the Divine Being from which we are derived and toward which we are directed. It is because we know what perfection is, however ill defined it may be for us, that we can never be satisfied with anything less. We are capable of transcending this world and thereby of exercising dominion over it because we already participate in the viewpoint of the transcendent source of all reality. We can be like gods in this world only because we are related to the true God who is over all. Our mastery is not our own. It is a sharing in his. Left to ourselves we are a sheer empty raging that oversteps all limits, very much like Nietzsche's "overman." We are utterly without direction.

Control Depends on Anchor in Beyond

Only if we have a point of reference beyond this world does our capacity for transcendence become a true governance of things. Without that transhuman origin and end we sink to the subhuman level of things. Without direction our transcendence means nothing. It is a vain flailing against all limits and finite satisfactions that has nothing to guide it but the momentary passions and impulses of our selves and the environment. Instead of being the masters of our fates we have become mere slaves of the forces around us. We are incapable of resisting the attractions and repulsions that buffet us. We are the tumbleweeds of history. The transcendent openness of human beings deprives them of any anchor in instinct or routine within nature. Deprived of its ultimate point of orientation, the world-transcending reach of humanity renders us the most defenseless of all creatures within existence. This is why we of all animals cannot be restrained within the natural limits, what Rudyard Kipling called the "law of the jungle." We will not confine ourselves to killing only what we can eat. We are consumed by an energy of excess that drives us beyond limits, and we are helpless to resist its deadly impulse.

Our power is powerless if there is no firm anchor that can hold it fast. Otherwise we are set loose on the vast ocean of reality. No matter how well equipped we may be or how capable we may be at traveling as we choose, we are as helpless as any little twig adrift on a great river so long as we have no direction in which to go. Technical power is only of benefit so long as we have a purpose for its use. Otherwise it is of no service to us and we are the passive victims of the forces of our own natures and the external circumstances in which we happen to be. It is not enough to talk about our choice of values as sufficient to guide us, for the language of subjective choice is merely a polite cover for the total moral ignorance that afflicts us. Values that are chosen are based on nothing more ultimate than our own subjective whim or inclination. Again, we are at the mercy of the currents that happen to buffet us at any given time. There is neither constancy nor direction to the exercise of our powers. More than ever we recognize our incapacity to live without a horizon of meaning.

The difficulty is that the meaning is always beyond us; otherwise we find that it is beneath our real aspirations as human beings. Almost as soon as a highest purpose is proposed to us, we become aware of the objections that assail it. Even if it is merely to live a happy and healthy life, we ask Why? What is the purpose of that? And the so-called transcendent purposes, such as service to God or humanity, fare no better. We still want to know why they are so valuable that they must be placed first. They too must be measured in their goodness. But it is here in that last turn or question that the real disclosure takes place. We must not stop the meditation at what looks like the perennial dead end of the "wise-guy" question. We are all familiar with the adolescent type who attempts to put a stop to every series of reflections by wanting the last reason justified to him. Why must we obey God, then, or why must we love one another? These are questions that have no answers, we recognize, not because there is no answer, but because the answer cannot be expressed in a way that will be invulnerable to a repetition of the question. Their answer lies not within the realm of immanence, but in the transcendent fullness that is the source of all value.

The questions themselves point us in the same direction. We cannot be satisfied with any immanent final purpose because we cannot conceive a limit to our aspirations. Whatever limit is proposed to us we still want to know what is beyond it. We want to know for any goal we are told to serve whether *it* is good. Any highest good confronts the scrutiny of goodness too. But instead of despairing at finding any account of our goal, as we so often do at this point in the meditation, we should recognize that we are not far from the kingdom of God. We are not satisfied with any immanent goal because once it is named, even calling it God, it becomes immanent and a target for the transcending finality of our souls. Once it is formulated it becomes vulnerable to critique. This is the insight of Buddhism, which resolutely refuses to name the highest reality in order to better ensure our chances of reaching it. We can make use of the same insight by recognizing the source of the endlessly questioning critique within us. We always ask Is it true? or Is it good? because we measure all in relation to the transcendent sense that is the deepest source of ourselves and yet beyond all formulation to ourselves.

The transcendent escapes all attempts to capture it, but it is the source of all attempts to realize it. It is that which measures all goods but which itself can never be measured. We continue to live within a horizon and no matter how far we travel toward it, the horizon remains constant. No amount of effort can enable us to leap over it. That embracing arch of mystery is the reassuring and impenetrable presence surrounding all that we do. It remains our ultimate frame of reference, yet always escapes our attempts to capture it. Human existence is inescapably structured by its openness toward mystery. We can never overleap our place within a whole that is transparent to us through our consciousness of it. For we do not merely live within a cosmos, as the Greeks called it, but we live consciously toward its reality. This is both the agony and the ecstasy of our lives. We cannot jump out of our place within the all, escape the human condition, to view the meaning of everything from the viewpoint of God. In this recognition we are released from the crushing prospect of thinking that we have understood it all and have encountered the limits. We continue to live in an unlimited horizon, toward a reality that is vastly beyond our human existence. We are guarded by mystery.

This is emphatically not a horizon of emptiness. For then we would be faced with an infinity of sameness. This is the great disillusion that faces us in the venture of space exploration. We will discover after traveling to or probing the outer reaches of the universe that we have merely changed location. We have not encountered the higher and more eminent reality that drew us on the search. What keeps us going, by contrast, is the aspiration toward that much greater reality that is qualitatively beyond us. We are not fired up by the thought of the endless sameness of space. Our spirit wants to go beyond all limits, and that aspiration has its source in the awareness of that for which it is in search. There would be no ceaseless human quest that remains ever unsatisfied with all its attainments, if there were not an intimation of a fullness of reality that lies beyond all limits. We are not surrounded by an infinity of emptiness, because that would never draw us in movement toward itself. We would just remain what we are where we are, if we sensed that all life is uniformly the same. It is rather the hunger for transcendent reality that is already glimpsed that constitutes the core of all our striving.

That limitless thrusting and being drawn is both the source of all the vitality of human life and the defining character of our freedom. We are free because we are directed beyond any finite achievements in this life. Our natures are not fixed because they cannot be confined within any specified limits. As soon as a limit is proposed, we aspire to the good that lies beyond it. We are in process, and what we are to be has never been definitively fixed. No matter what a person does or what he becomes, he remains free and no one can say that he cannot undergo a change of heart. All our contracts and commitments are made in the "fear and trembling" uncertainty that we will be unable to sustain them. We can never pass a definitive judgment on the worth of a person. In other words, a human being never reaches the point in this life where we can say that what he or she is is unalterably fixed and forever. This is the same thing as saying that we are free. What we are is a process, and remaining true to our commitments is a process of remaining true. We can never simply relax in an accomplishment that is secure. In every moment we remain free, although never utterly free of all direction.

Freedom without direction would be a mere empty purposelessness, little distinguishable from a sheer flailing around. No, what makes freedom of such value to us is that it is the process by which we are connected to the transcendent. Freedom is of value to human beings because it is the means by which they realize the highest. Without that higher level of reality, to which we are drawn and by which we are measured, it would have none of the dignity that marks it as the core dimension of our humanity. What point would there be to the protection of human freedom, the elaborate safeguards to ensure that individuals give their informed consent to all that involves them, if freedom itself was merely a matter of following the vacuity of our whims? Surely it is because freedom is oriented toward the awesomeness of transcendent reality that the sanctity of its end attaches to this human capacity itself. Even when we no longer clearly believe in a transcendent destiny for human life, we cannot shake the immense dignity pervading human freedom. We continue to regard it as the most sacrosanct area of the person. Within that profound intimation is implanted the awareness of the reality that endows human freedom with its irreproachable dignity and indispensability.

When we think of the action of Maximilian Kolbe who stepped out of the selection line in Auschwitz to take the place of a fellow camp inmate, marching off to die in his place, we cannot but wonder at the force of human freedom. Nothing can withstand it because it is the means by which a human being takes his stand toward the good that lies beyond all measure. What makes freedom so important is that it is our capacity to lay hold of transcendent goodness. Not only would it serve no purpose if there was not such an horizon of transcendent goodness drawing us, but we would hardly even be free at all. If we are not responding to the pull of a transcendent reality, then we are being drawn toward the multiplicity of merely physical and psychical realities that surround us. In a sense we are failing to exercise our freedom and giving in to the immediate impulses that happen to dominate in the struggle to control us at any particular moment. Real freedom, in contrast, is always an orientation beyond the merely immediate and in relation to what is enduringly of value. This does not mean that we can escape the necessity of ministering to our immediate needs as human beings, only that such immediate pursuits must never be allowed to define us. To the extent that we have become merely a consumer of food or a client of gratification, then we have lost our humanity. We become human beings only by virtue of our capacity to direct our lives in reference to that transcendent fulfillment that lies beyond all finite satisfactions.

Success in this project of becoming who we are hangs on our capacity to follow the deepest intimations within ourselves. Even in an age that seems to have lost any clear sense of direction, we are not individually relieved of the responsibility for who we are. There is more at stake here than the future of history or the fate of our era. It is our very selves that hangs in the balance. Worse than the failure of an age, we are in danger of losing our souls, a value that is beyond all finite historical achievement. It is in response to that challenge that I write the present book. I offer it as part of the effort to find real personal meaning in human life despite the disintegration of the civilization in which we live. The opening to hope that it offers is derived from the discovery that the widespread collapse of meaning we observe around us need not be such an unlimited disaster. From another point of view it may be seen as a blessing. Rather than seeing the failure of all public philosophies as the end of man's search for meaning, we will view it as the beginning of the truly genuine search for truth. Instead of looking for meaning in formulas and conceptions, we can direct our attention to their source in the limitless aspirations of human life itself. Rather than searching for a false fulfillment, we can look toward the only one that can really answer our unlimited longing. The collapse of all finite satisfactions prepares us for the rediscovery of the reality that was the ultimate source of their attraction. To this meditation we now turn.

CHAPTER 2

PERSON AS PROCESS

W E ALL hate to be labeled. As soon as someone begins to pin us down as just a _____ we feel the resistance rising within us. We are repelled by the idea that we might be reducible to such a simplistic classification, because we know we are so much more. Even if someone attempted to make an exhaustive list of all the qualities that apply to us and even if they did an accurate job, we would still escape the attempt at definition. We all believe that there is more to us than even we ourselves can fully articulate, so much more that life is not long enough to complete the inventory. Each of us, we sense, is inexhaustible. When the media or social experts reduce us to the crude racial and economic categories of their jargon, we are offended because we know they have missed the reality of our lives. Such classifications may be useful in dealing with strangers, but they are only the outer shell of the inner human beings we know in our lives. We are repulsed by the suggestion that we can be explained in such one-dimensional terms.

Social classifications fly in the face of everything we know about ourselves and sense in one another. They miss the central realization that we are incomplete. No matter how much we have attained or where we might be on some scale of measurement, we have already gone beyond them. We slip the net of limitations because we are forever moving forward. What purports to define us—our age, our income, our talents, our possessions—are all in the past, and we are already looking back at them from a viewpoint further along in life. There is nothing that can capture who we are because we are perpetually outside of what determines us. The image that best depicts a human life is a journey or a pilgrimage. We are continuously in movement, leaving behind what is fixed and quantifiable and moving on to the unknown and the undefined. Human life cannot be captured in a summation; it can only be recorded in a narrative.

Our odyssey is fundamentally open-ended. We do not have a predetermined plan, nor are we following any automatic mechanism. Who we are remains for us to determine and it is unfolded as we daily and inexorably live our lives. There is no fixed nature with laws of operation built in. Human being is a process or a project, and it is up to each one of us to take charge of its development. We are responsible. We are free. Who we are has not yet been completed and we are charged with the responsibility for guiding the determination of what we are to become. We create ourselves, not in the sense that we are the source of our own existence and that our powers are unlimited, but in the sense that we participate in the work of self-creation. That is the source of the dignity by which we surpass all other realities we know.

Acting for Reasons

Physics, chemistry, biology, and animal psychology deal with forces and things that are ever the same, that exercise no role in shaping their destiny. Planets and atoms, organisms and instincts are invariant and recurrent in their operations. Regarding such things, generalizations are easy and predictions are reliable because they follow laws over which such entities have no choice. By contrast, human beings are notoriously difficult to study. Unlike astronomers who plot Haley's comet, which they know will return in another seventy-five years, I cannot predict where my son will be in the next seventy-five minutes. The reason is that, short of constraining him by physical force, I must rely on his free cooperation. Even in the presence of an impressive array of inducements both positive and negative, that dependence on his free self-direction is bound to result in a significant degree of variability. And that is on a good day. To treat him in any other way than as responsible for himself is to look on him as less than a human being.

A radical mistake is made every time we imagine that the methods used for studying nature can be applied to human nature. There is all the difference in the world between entities that have no choice but to follow the exigencies of their nature, and beings whose nature it is to intelligently participate in the shaping of their own nature. All that the methods of natural science can yield are the external dimensions of their lives. The inner reality escapes because it consists of the reasons and the reasoning by which they arrived at the choices they have made. That is what we have to understand if we are to understand who they are. What persuaded them to do the things they do? We may not find their reasons very cogent (they may not in fact be very convincing), but we cannot deny that they are the sort of beings who act because of reasons. Nothing compels them. They can only act out of reasons and motives they themselves find persuasive.

Understanding human beings always means taking their own explanations seriously. What were the reasons they found compelling or the motives to which they yielded? To understand another person is never to reduce them to the observable factors of their environment. It is to enter into the inner world of their free self-direction, a world that has no other structure than the intimations they find plausible to follow. So-called objective factors have a role to play, but never a decisive role. Always what decides the issue is what this particular person accepts as decisive. The only avenue into that inner world is the reasoning process they are capable of articulating for themselves and for others. The understanding of human beings must always begin with their self-understanding. That may be erroneous, biased, and ineffective, but there is no denying that their actions were undertaken for some such reasons. They did not act as automata. To the extent that they were the actions of conscious human beings they were chosen more or less intelligently. That is the point of reference for our conversation with them.

What makes us sanguine that we will be able to unravel the meaning of their actions through conversation? Admittedly, it is unlikely that we will ever be able to give a full account of the reasoning and motivation for actions, whether our own or those of others. But we are both conscious. That means that we are capable of stepping outside of what we have said or done and examining it further. We can subject our reasoning and our choosing to critical scrutiny and proceed to evaluate and reevaluate our actions until we are sufficiently satisfied. There is nothing that stands in the way of our free deliberation because, for any potential limit to the process of deliberation, we can always evaluate its capacity to terminate the process. Nothing can call a halt to our free deliberation but the process of deliberation itself. We must be persuaded or admit the termination. Nothing extraneous can provide a reason. All reasoning is from within.

Thus freedom is our capacity to always examine ourselves critically from a stage beyond whatever stage we have reached. No matter how far our deliberation has progressed, it can only be terminated by what convinces us. There is no other stopping point, unless we are compelled to stop from outside, because we are always capable of asking the reason for our last reason. Only what we can regard as a sufficient reason can terminate the process of self-reflection. That is, our actions and choices are inherently the fruit of free deliberation because we are always capable of examining them and being examined on them. We can discuss our actions because we are able to step outside them. I am always more than the sum total of what I have done and said because I can always look back at that totality. In that way I am *always* more than the sum. That is what being conscious and intelligent is all about. We are free because we are ever capable of considering our own process of considering. Nothing can interrupt the process except our own free choice, which we expect to terminate in what is reasonable.

We may not always live up to that high expectation of reasonableness. Indeed, many of our actions are confined to the routine. Very often we go through the motions of our day without really thinking. Who needs to think about eating his breakfast or catching the train? But that does not mean we could not give reasons for them if we were asked or that we would be surprised if someone pointed out what we were doing. We are not sleepwalking. But to the extent that our actions approach such an autonomic state, to the extent that reflection is less necessary in initiating them, to that extent they can be captured within the categories of behavioral science. The social sciences do succeed in describing the large parts of our world in which we do proceed unthinkingly, driven more by inertia or routine or the unexamined impulse of prejudice. But they miss the deeper meaning of such phenomena. That can only be yielded up to the investigator who asks us to consider the reason why we are doing what we do, or compels us to acknowledge that we are bereft of sufficiently plausible justifications.

Freedom for Community

It is the same capacity to reflect on who we are that saves us from definitive identification with our failures. We may not have lived up to our calling to follow reason. Passion and prejudice may have truncated the process of deliberation. Our reasoning may have yielded to the irrational. But we are not trapped forever in that condition. The very fact that we can ask ourselves or be asked by others why we did such-and-such renders us free from the final enclosement within ourselves. We are capable of love because we are capable of living beyond ourselves. I can think of you as you think of yourself. I can love another person for his or her own sake, not for my good. The pressures and demands that arise from my immediate needs have a major role in shaping how I view the world. If I am in pain or driven by self-desire, it will be very hard for me to see your point of view, but I am not incapable of seeing it. Why? Because no matter how consumed I am by my own preoccupations, the fact that they are consciously and intelligently pursued means that they are already subject to my reflexive control. I am aware of what I am doing and in this awareness can move beyond doing it. That is what my freedom means.

Nature is what is given and fixed. My self-direction means that I am continuously engaged in a consideration of how far the givenness of nature should be allowed to control the outcome. Suppose that I am in a rage because everything has gone wrong since I got up this morning, and now the car has broken down just when I needed it most. Should I vent my wrath on the nearest thing I can hit or should I find a way of bringing it under control? Whatever I do, I know it is my doing. I have deliberately chosen the response. In the deepest sense the real me is the inexhaustible capacity to go beyond the condition of the moment. I can consider it. I am not locked up within my skin, but capable of reaching out limitlessly to the rest of the world. There is no barrier to the movement of my sympathy because for every limit I can ask, What is beyond it? This is what makes community possible between human beings. Their communication arises in a concrete physical setting but it is not simply exhausted by those conditions. I may not be a very good practitioner of universal love but there is no necessary obstacle in the way to my eventual practice of such love.

There is even a strong predisposition that intermittently succeeds in breaking through my selfishness. What, after all, is my capacity to consider other people if not the awareness that there is no limit, short of the whole of human life, at which my sympathy might stop. There is no good other than the highest good that my striving should serve. Any lesser good or any reduced expectation automatically calls forth the question Why? Why give only this much and no more? Why stop at this point and not that one? Why love only this neighbor and not that one? Every arbitrary restriction of the range of my understanding and love begs the question of its rationale. To the extent that we become aware that all such restrictions represent a failure to love, we find ourselves drawn into the struggle to painfully enlarge the freedom of our hearts. The capacity to step outside of ourselves that is at the core of our self-creation turns out to have an in-built finality within it.

Fulfillment Transcendent

The direction can only be defined as transcendent. It has no inherent stopping point short of the All. Whatever limitation is proposed, we spontaneously seek to transcend it. Naturally our energy, our interest, and our resources are all limited by the circumstances of our lives. We are not pure spirits capable of soaring as far as the illumination draws us. Our spirits are embodied, and often heavily encumbered by the limited range of our physical capacities. But we recognize such limitations for what they are: the accidental circumstances of our lives. The attendant baggage does not invalidate the direction of the principle we also experience directly as the dynamic of our lives. Nothing short of universal openness and love will satisfy the thirst of our souls. There is a big gap between attainment and aspiration, but we cannot collapse the one into the other. That would result either in the hypocrisy of claiming to have reached perfection or in the abandonment of all attempts to live beyond self-centered gratification.

Authenticity demands that we recognize the tension as the inescapable condition of our lives. We must struggle between unlimited aspiration and limited attainment, without either despairing or rejecting the incompleteness of our lives. At its deepest level our freedom is dependent on the preservation of that tension. It is not merely our capacity to view ourselves from outside that constitutes our freedom. More than simply the fact that everything purporting to determine our decisions can become an object of scrutiny and reflection, more than simply the distance we are capable of establishing between ourselves and any putative state we have reached, more even than the ceaseless dynamic of our questioning self-examinations, there is the underlying thrust that keeps the entire process in motion. Why are we best defined as beings in the process of defining themselves? Well, it can only be because we are incapable of ever reaching our fulfillment. All that we know is finite, limited, and ultimately dissatisfying. Our disposition is toward the infinite bliss of perfection.

What preserves the ceaseless dynamism of our consciousness is, in other words, our transcendent orientation. Without that limitless thrust we would hardly be drawn into the restless unsatisfying search for fulfillment. Sooner or later we would have settled down within the routine whose satisfactions are scarcely above the animal level. Isn't this what is so thoroughly disdained in those human beings who seem to have accepted such a subhuman existence? Caricatures like "Joe Six-Pack" come to mind. Freedom is, after all, not just a capacity. Unlike money, which can be left in the bank, freedom that is not exercised eventually disappears. What is it, then, that propels us to use it, that maintains us in the tension of striving without reaching the goal? To the extent that we live more and more within a leisured consumer society, ministering without strain to our many wants, the temptation to settle down in somnolent indulgence is becoming more of a problem. There is a real danger of the loss of freedom to desuetude, although it is never likely to be realized completely. The sting of dissatisfaction reminds us of the higher calling toward which we must exercise ourselves.

In many ways the worst thing that could happen to us would be to see the dream of modern technology reach its goal. The comprehensive ordering of all things, so that our every need was gratified almost before we became aware of it, would dampen rather than enlarge the range of our freedom. Compelled to reflect less and less on the obstacles to be surmounted in life, we would become more and more the passive products of forces beyond ourselves. Without the need to think, we would be reduced to the level of instruments. The improbability or even the impossibility of technology successfully ministering to all of our needs does not obviate the danger of this tendency. It still works to undermine the expectation that strain and struggle is the destiny of humankind, and encourages the illusion that we might eventually escape the tension. Lost in this dream is the sense of the irreplaceable value of self-responsibility. That is a treasure preserved by the consciousness for which we can never find a resting place in anything within this life.

We are engaged in the process of enacting and disclosing who we are because we are never completed. If it were possible for us to reach a stage beyond which we did not aspire to go, then we would no longer engage in the struggle for self-realization. There would be no goal and therefore no striving to reach that goal. Without its exercise freedom would be no more. Our lives would have shrunk to the level of things whose reality is whole and complete here and now. Freedom exists only for beings who must separate themselves from all that they are in actualizing what they are to become. It is not merely consciousness that guarantees the viability of freedom. It is the larger tension within which consciousness exists that prevents it from collapsing in on itself. Instead of shrinking into the gravitational blackness from which not even light can emerge, human consciousness is drawn into the radiance of that greater reality that is the evanescent goal forever on its horizon. We exist in tension toward a goal that as soon as it exists is no longer a goal. Our telos remains the ever-present nonpresent beyond.

This formulation is deliberately awkward because it is impossible to express transcendent reality. Once it is given a name it is no longer quite so transcendent. Certainly, it has acquired a more tangible presence within this world. That is necessary and inevitable if we want to refer to it at all, but it also makes it a target for our world-transcending drive. Anything that has become simply part of the world has already lost its transcendent power and is subjected to the same scrutinizing dissatisfaction as everything else that is part of the world. We will not be satisfied with anything less than the truly beyond. This is the deepest component of modern atheism. It is not that the modern secular world has lost all sense of the divine, but that it cannot recognize the traditional God of revelation as its transcendent goal. The God of Christianity or Judaism has become too immanent. Today he is a part of history and almost by definition cannot be a part of the mysterious beyond.

The horizon of mystery that guards and draws us cannot be named without losing its place and becoming enclosed in a further horizon. The nature of the horizon is that it cannot be reached. We can arrive at a place, but never at the horizon itself. That would be to step out of our position, to cease to be human beings, and to become the source of the horizon itself. But nothing would be served by such an attempt since merely asserting it does not change our position in reality. No, our problem remains the age-old one of attuning our lives to the only transcendent reality there is, at the border of our consciousness, and thereby gaining whatever participation in higher meaning it is possible for a human being to attain. Much of the modern world can be interpreted as an attempt to regain the transparence of that transcendent meaning within a context where the traditional symbolizations have become opaque.

Modern Misdirection of Quest

Rather than looking on our own time as an era of atheism, skepticism, and relativism, we might equally view it as an age marked by a new outburst of faith in the transcendent mystery that guards the integrity of our existence. The very extent to which the traditional religious symbols have been subjected to relentless critique is itself a reflection of the same faith. Nietzsche understood this paradox and agonized over its consequences. He sought in vain to obliterate the faith that he knew was the source of his own critique. For what is the analysis of the mendacity of Christian morality if itself not an expression of the same morality? Nietzsche maintained that Christianity died under the impact of its own moral scrutiny, that it negated itself, but what is that but testament to the vitality of the same moral conviction? The reason why so many of the secular messiahs, such as Marx or Comte or Freud, sound like Old Testament prophets is that they derive their moral authority from the same source. Thinking they have undermined the revelatory tradition through its own imperious demands, they have borne witness to the inescapability of those very same convictions.

This is a realization that has dawned on the more perceptive of the contemporary successors of the tradition of critique. Deconstructionists, who are synonymous with the relativization of all meaning, have belatedly come to acknowledge that their own practice does derive from something, although not from a specifiable complex of meaning. For anyone with an ear for such dimensions, this had been clear all along. Why spend one's life assiduously pointing out the incoherences within the entire Western tradition, laying the burden of suspicion on the entire project of philosophical and theological meaning, if one is not aching with the need to make contact with what is beyond all doubt? There is a distinct tone of protesting too much in their entire laborious exposition. Even the suggestion that meaning is relative is somehow parasitical on the notion of what is not relative. The judgment of relativity is measured by the notion of what cannot be charged with that deficiency.

What is true in the deconstructionists' critique and what they have succeeded in making clearer than ever is that all historical meaning is contingent. For any principle we may care to enunciate, we can examine its economic, social, psychological, symbolic, and political sources and even conclude that it is never quite what it purports to be. The hermeneutics of suspicion, by which articulations of meaning are recognized as most often serving the interests of the powerful, can marshal an impressive body of evidence in its favor. To that extent we might even note that the critique itself is less novel than it claims to be. Few of the great thinkers of history would be surprised by its suggestion. But what is most significant is the unspoken and unexamined perspective from which the critique is launched. By any plausible account, the hermeneutics of suspicion can only turn its probing gaze on the injustice of history so long as it preserves the notion of what a fairer and truer rendering of things would be. There cannot be a judgment of exploitation if there is not the sense of the nonexploitative standard by which it is measured. Suspicion of falsehood depends on the notion of truth. The problem always is how to articulate that notion of truth or justice in such a way that it escapes the effect of the same critique. Deconstructionists may be identified as those who have abandoned the attempt and concluded that the task is impossible. Hence their conclusion that there cannot be any meaning, despite their own reliance on the contrary in their critique.

Yet despite the inconsistencies of the contemporary brand of deconstructionism, their critique cannot be dismissed out of hand. Nor can they themselves be dislodged through the accusation of self-contradiction. How can that disturb those who have already admitted that the quest for meaning is an illusion or worse? No, the real strength of the deconstructionist position derives from the sense of what must lie beyond all contingent meaning. It is another form of meditation on the horizon of transcendent mystery that guards and grounds all that we do. That is the value of deconstructionism. It testifies to the dissatisfaction with all finite contingent frames of reference, a dissatisfaction that will not permit us to rest within any purely immanent construction. As soon as a candidate is proposed, we immediately rush to know what is beyond the putative limits and to expose the degree to which they fall short of embodying the transcendent goal. Deconstructionism does no more than raise the perennial restlessness of the human spirit into a theoretical stance. Even without the philosophical encouragement, we are familiar with the instability of all historical efforts to fix the flow of presence. The tendency for meaning to drain away or be coopted in some ulterior function is well known.

No sanctuary exists to preserve the life of meaning within history. Once articulated it escapes the living tension toward transcendence and cannot avoid the fate of becoming embroiled in all the contingencies of history. But that does not mean that we must conclude that the project of uncovering and recovering meaning is an impossibility. There is still the possibility from which the meaning originated in the first place, that is, within the existential tension toward transcendent reality that is lived prior to all attempts to capture it in symbols. It is the presence of that living tension within the deconstructionists that is the source of their critique and it is the assurance that the exercise of critique might yield more than the futility of a game. While it may not lead to a new exposition of meaning, it contains the promise of something even higher. The meditation on the incapacity of all finite symbols to contain the fullness of meaning keeps alive the touch of that transcendent presence as the abiding horizon of the quest. It is the sense of contact with that other reality beyond all finitude that is the sustaining source of the whole effort.

The more one examines it, the more it is apparent that the so-called secular world is not really secular at all. Simply because it no longer explicitly takes its point of reference from divine reality, as medieval Christian civilization did, does not mean that the influence of transcendent reality is any less present. It is still not a closed universe because human beings are constitutionally incapable of living within it. Every fiber of their being reaches toward a horizon that is beyond all that they are and all that they have accomplished. When the language of religion is no longer normative, other dimensions of life begin to play the role of standing for the beyond. We will reflect later on the problems that such misplacements are likely to cause, but for the moment all we need to note is their source. There would be no such transfers of significance, human beings would be perfectly content to live within the animal limits of their existence, if they did not carry within them the sense of unlimited aspiration toward the transcendent. The question toward which the entire reflection directs us is, What is the character of that longing? Is it based on anything real, does it derive from any independent reality? Or is it pure illusion?

We have already seen that the impossibility of reaching final and complete satisfaction is what makes freedom possible. If we were to reach a stage of contentment in which we could settle down without struggle or reflection, then there would no longer be any looking back on ourselves or any movement toward that which we are not yet. All would already be present. There would be no way to separate ourselves from what we are, and there would scarcely be any movement at all. Only if we have a perspective beyond all that we are or have attained can there be the conscious movement in which freedom is exercised. We can scarcely even conceive of self-reflection and self-realization except in light of the awareness of that which we are not. Without that sense of distance it would be impossible to distance ourselves from who we are. Like clams, we would be happy locked within the totality of the here-and-now. It is only if we are touched by the sense of what lies beyond all finite satisfactions that we can be sure we will not settle down within the dumbness of the wholly present.

What sustains the reality of freedom over a lifetime is the transcendent character of that dissatisfaction. No state of satiety can assuage it because it is oriented toward a fulfillment radically beyond all finite reality. Otherwise freedom would not be such a constant and, with freedom, there goes the entire restless expansion that is human history. We are endlessly on the move, and what sustains that movement is the incapacity of any of the intermediate stations to provide our final rest. Only beings driven by a longing out of this world could pour such ceaseless energies into this one. But more than the endless fecundity of human creativity is the dignity of the self-determination it represents. In engaging in the ceaseless reflection and work that creates a world, the preeminent reality is that such beings engage in the process of creating themselves. They are responsible for who they are. That is the dignity of human beings and the reason for their primacy within the order of things. Only self-determining beings deserve to be recognized as unlimited ends-in-themselves.

Previously we had said that the reason for the exalted position of man is that he is made in the image of God. He carries the spark of divinity within him. But what does that mean except that we are touched by the sense of a reality that transcends everything within this world? We are ever able to separate ourselves from what we have been and look toward what we might be because our standpoint is ultimately beyond everything finite. It is this that guarantees our freedom as an unending process of self-determination. We are never fully determined because our full actualization can only be reached in the reality that is beyond all questions. Whatever we do is measured in the light of that attraction that always remains brighter than the merely reflected light that all finite attainments carry for us. They may contain some of the promise of the transcendent good but what saves us from resting content with them is the presence of the mysterious pull beyond them. It is that imperious attraction that preserves our freedom.

Confirmation through Search

But, the objection arises, could this not all still be an illusion? Granted that freedom is sustained through the sense of dissatisfaction with any of the accomplishments reached, perhaps it is no more than a necessary illusion? Maybe it is even a dangerous illusion since it sets us up for disappointment and frustration. We look constantly for a transcendent fulfillment from things that are incapable of providing it. Perhaps it would be better to recognize the limits of our condition and accept the limited expectations that are possible. Why beat ourselves over the head pursuing the unattainable? Isn't this the neurosis of a religiously inspired civilization that asks men to frustrate their natural desires in the name of an unreal fulfillment? Even at the purely natural level we still have a great deal to do to avoid the distorting and disappointing illusions that attach to our aspirations. We must not only give up the idea of heaven but we must also be careful to abandon the idea of heaven on earth. That last refuge of the religious illusion still infects and prevents our efforts to reach the only satisfaction that is possible for human beings. We are only human. Why reach for anything higher and why not accept an order of limits?

There is no denying the power of this sentiment in our own age when all faiths, religious and secular, seem to have exhausted themselves. The only difficulty is that it is impossible. We may in a moment of depression declare our readiness to live without illusions, to accept the workaday satisfactions available to us, to moderate our expectations. But we cannot. Everything within us cries out at the absurdity of such a condition. Without the penumbra of a larger meaning beyond it even our everyday life shrinks to the intolerable confinement of a prison cell. We can imagine few things more oppressive than the endless futility of a life without the expansiveness of meaning. Why go on living? is, as Camus said, the first philosophical question generated when we are confronted with the absurd. If every day and every achievement promises no more than the emptiness of all we have known up to now, then there seems to be little to draw us forward. Why not give up now since we will have to give up later, with just as little to show for our efforts? The prospect of a life utterly drained of illumination from the beyond, however fleetingly connected, is a crushing realization.

The only possibility of sustaining the stance of living without hope is that we manage to suppress the questions. Of course, that is the advice of the antimetaphysical gurus who counsel us to forsake the search for higher meaning, since none is disclosed to us or at least none capable of winning authoritative consent. At best we might live within our private worlds. If we want to be honest, however, we should acknowledge the forlornness of our condition without attempting to disguise it with illusions. Why seek to deny the truth? If we cannot find our way to that higher meaning that would make sense of our lives, then we can at least live with the nobility of those who refuse to lie. Some elemental sense of dignity calls us to place forthrightness above even our own happiness. Besides, what value is happiness purchased at the price of self-deception? They will prove to be equally counterfeit. At the end of it all we may not have gained entry into the gates of paradise but, in another sense, we have gained much more: we have gained our dignity as human beings whose fidelity to the truth transcends even their own existence.

But . . . isn't this what we mean by the touch of a higher reality? What is it that draws us in the direction of transcendent truth, the resolution to strip away all falsehood, to live without reliance on anything except the pure strength of honesty? Nothing except the sense that this is the most real reality there is. In comparison with it nothing else—our comfort, our reassurance, our self-esteem—matters. They are the mere dross of life in contrast to the durability of truth. Everything else passes away; only the path of fidelity to the truth endures. It is the way that puts us in contact with the only reality there is. Even if it is the admission that we are irrevocably cut off from a paradise of meaning, then the unflinching recognition of that truth is itself the means of living the highest life possible for us to attain. Against either the dissolution of pleasure or the futility of illusion, we follow the intimations of the higher way. If paradise is closed to us, we can still live by its perfume.

In this meditation we wonder if indeed it was not always thus with human beings. Perhaps we in the late modern world suffer under the greatest illusion of all, that the solidity of meaning so confidently transmitted from the past was based on the same slender thread. The more we reflect on it, the more we realize that it could hardly be otherwise. Theological or cultural meaning that seemed to possess the massiveness of an order impervious to human frailty and variability was really suspended in the air. They were held up because a great many human beings sensed within them the transcendent touch they knew within their own hearts. The transcendent itself could not be represented. By definition it lies beyond all definition as the ever-present nonpresent at the border of all human experience. It casts its radiance over all other reality but is not itself a part of that reality. What is so different about our own contemporary pursuit of the intimations of the real beyond the boundaries of the absurd?

While we never succeed in jumping into the beyond that draws us, we also never fail to sense its presence as the inexorable undertow of our lives. Human life continues to be led, as Plato observed, in a "between" state of existence. The tension has neither been abolished nor escaped. If it were, then human life and the freedom of self-determination that characterizes it would be no more. We can neither sink to the level of immanent realities that are wholly present, to live as unreflectively as a stone or a frog, nor can we leap into the fullness of the reality that is not present, to live in the possession of unending perfection. Our fate is to remain within the poles of that tension, and it is its very irresolvability that constitutes the restless free creativity that is human history. Our situation today is unchanged except that we are less likely to recognize the transcendent pole that draws us. We are more inclined to regard that as the realm of illusion. Nothing is changed by the shift of accent, although it does make a difference to our self-understanding and consequently to the response to our condition. We will examine this problem further in Chapter 4 on religion. For the moment all we need to recognize is that the tension toward the transcendent continues even in the face of its explicit denial.

The question of its illusory character is moot since it is the very same openness to truth beyond all construction that is the criterion we use in judging what is false. Without the sense of what is true without reservation or equivocation we could scarcely engage in the reflection. What else is capable of sustaining our quest for the truth, that absolutely will not permit us to settle for some soothing platitudes, that pushes us on relentlessly until we reach our goal of the unimpeachedly authentic reality? Whence originates that drive if not in the sense of our transcendent finality? No matter what the limitations proposed or how plausible the resting place presented, our unlimited openness will categorically refuse to tolerate its inhibition. We can neither accept any goal short of the totality nor deny the validity of our quest as illusory. Our lives are constituted by the movement toward reality beyond whatever stage we have reached, and the process as a whole is destined to continue inexorably until it reaches the final goal of the transcendent fullness of all reality.

Even the suggestion that we might not reach that transcendent fulfillment is not enough to undermine the movement. That is because the quest is not based on the expectation of collecting on a promise in the future. Discussion of an afterlife is very often couched in terms of a mere prolongation of our life here. This has much to do with why the topic has lost its appeal in the modern world. We are, after all, capable of extending our longevity here and are still working on it. No, our interest is in the higher or more real life. We already know what everyday life is like; our attraction is toward what transcends that possibility. This is the core of the relentlessly transcendent drive of the human spirit, which is as much in evidence today as in any age. Skepticism about the afterlife or our final fulfillment is all beside the point. We know in our own experience the movement toward higher life. To the extent that we respond to the transcendent pull we know it directly. We already begin to live it, and so the question of its truth value is irrelevant. We know it is true because we experience it as a more real life than any other. Even if we were told that truth lies in some other direction, we would refuse it because we already glimpse the higher reality by which it must be measured.

Our freedom is not empty. Contrary to the common perception that we are engaged in making abstract choices between discrete alternatives, the unfolding self-realization of human life is imbued with its inner sense of direction. We are not without a rudder or a compass. Even before we reach it, we know the destination we seek because in some sense we are already there. Otherwise how would it be possible to reach any goal? We would not know when we had attained it if we did not begin with some sense of it. This is even more the case with the overall direction of life which is the embracing horizon within which our freedom is exercised. Without such knowledge, then, we would never be able to order our search, and without the recognition of its transcendent goal we would never understand the insatiable character of freedom. But all of that is available once we meditate on the nature of the impulse that moves us. The ceaseless character of our striving and the direction by which it should be ordered are clarified only by the knowledge from which they begin.

There would be no movement at all unless there was the awareness of dissatisfaction. We know that we fall short. Our deficiency must be made up by straining toward that which has more, toward a level of life and meaning beyond what we possess. Moreover, we know that the immediate object toward which we move is itself deficient. It is incapable of satisfying all our aspirations. It is limited. Throwing ourselves upon a succession of such objects merely results in a serialized acknowledgment of dissatisfaction. Eventually we are brought to recognize that our longing is not to be assuaged by any or all of the objects of our acquaintance. It is a longing for another higher reality. But which one? Surely it must be for that which is the final and complete possession of all perfection, that beyond which nothing more can be desired. We know transcendent being in this sense because it is that which is present as the presence that will not permit us to rest content within any finite satisfactions. It is there as the unspoken irritant in all our aspirations.

Without that recognition the exercise of freedom in a ceaseless quest of impossible satiety is doomed both to frustration and un-intelligibility. Only if we understand how much this world and its pleasures fall short of our true fulfillment can we really enjoy them on their own terms. We will return to this theme of the spiritual person as the only one who is truly at home in the world in Chapter 5. For now we merely note it in passing as we recognize its centrality in unraveling the nature of human freedom that derives from the unending incompleteness of the person. We are a process of self-enactment and self-disclosure whose freedom is guaranteed by its incapacity to reach its final realization. But it is only if we understand the character of its transcendent goal that we can avoid the sense that "the expense of spirit in a waste of shame is lust in action" (Shakespeare, Sonnet 129). Not only does the recognition of freedom depend on the radically transcendent orientation of the person, but its exercise can only acquire direction from the same understanding of the structure constituting it.

The process of the person is not a sheer activity. It has a direction that unfolds from the orientation toward its final goal. The differentiation of our transcendent goal not only relieves all the intermediate pursuits of the impossible burden of finality, it also provides an order within which they can be related to the whole. The luminosity of the end casts its radiated light over the whole of human life. This is what provides the means of weighing different values. A scale of measurement is possible only in relation to a principle untouched by any suggestion of the arbitrary. By viewing all things in the perspective of the final end, participation in the highest reality there is, we can take their true measure. Such is the order constituted by the recognition of the transcendent finality of human freedom. Through it we apprehend the abiding process of self-creation that is the character of the person, the distinction between our final goal and the finite character of all intermediate goals, and the means by which they can be ordered as values on the way toward that which is the source of all value.

The recognition of the transcendent openness that is human freedom is essential to its proper unfolding. Only by recognizing its transcendent finality can we understand all intermediate structures for what they are without railing against their nothingness. The relentless critique of all intervening stages and definitions, most recently by the deconstructionists, is in large part prompted by the same unlimited longing. Everything falls short, everything proves imperfect in relation to the transcendent reality glimpsed within. We have seen that this is the infinity of human freedom that guarantees the unreachability of any finite nature within this life. The process of human self-determination will continue without ceasing because it is drawn by a goal that is beyond all goals attainable. But instead of concluding that human life is thereby condemned to the burden of an impossible freedom driven toward an unreachable goal, we have seen that it is this tension that constitutes its supreme dignity and provides the way for our participation in that higher life. The tension is irresolvable and inescapable. Only by playing our part in the drama we are charged in part with creating can we attain to anything of value in our lives.

The attempt to reject our part within the transcendent mystery is an impossibly contradictory suggestion. It cannot secure any other values, indifference to meaning, for example, because all other values are dependent on the unfillable openness of who we are. Without such transcendent openness human freedom would have a limit. The project of self-creation would have an end. After that freedom would be no more, since it would no more be needed. Everything depends on the recognition of the tension within which we find ourselves. If we forget the touch of our transcendent goal, then the meaning of all intermediate goals evaporates. We find ourselves in the wasteland of nihilism. If we focus too insistently on the attainment of our final fulfillment in the here-and-now, then we will distort the meaning of all lesser goods. Placing an impossible burden of ultimacy on them, we will expend our lives to no purpose. Either way we will have lost the thread of meaning that draws us. We can only find our way by holding firmly to its gentle pull, neither forcing nor ignoring its guidance. The mystery of our freedom is that we are partners in a drama whose meaning we are enacting. The success of the enterprise depends on our willingness to play our part without seeking to abolish or dominate the whole. It is in this supreme drama of the moral life that we gain or lose our very selves.

CHAPTER 3

MORAL TRUTH IN ACTION

T ALK OF the undetermined creativity of our freedom runs the risk of suggesting that it is a pure possibility. Our lives are a blank paper on which we may allow the unrestrained play of our imagination. As the innocent guardians of whimsy we may give free reign to our creativity. This charming misconception has an undoubted appeal to the cultural heirs of romanticism. Our predilection toward boundless self-expression, the celebration of our endlessly unique diversities, and the unquestioned primacy of freedom over evaluation of achievements all dispose in that direction. Unfettered subjectivity crowds out all suggestion of authoritative models of order. Classical conceptions of order cannot withstand the romantic avocation of individuality. Our whole moral outlook is shaped by the same pervasive subjectivity; the identification of the person as a process of self-enactment seems to play directly into such proclivities. Are we condemned to the interminable inanities of self-improvers?

This question already alerts us to the problem. It would be hard to imagine anything more oppressive than the endless search for oneself in the vacuum of subjectivity. What would become of us wandering without direction in the wasteland of the pure "I"? Lost in the cosmos of the ego, we would be destined to lurch from one passion to another, under the infatuation of now one guru, now another, ever the helpless playthings of the shifting winds of fashion and fad. In the excessively leisured West, we might come to resemble caricatures of ourselves. Self-help books and the therapeutic professions would dominate our lives. All are embraced in the bright promise of fulfillment and as quickly discarded as the false prophets of disappointment. What could be more pathetic? Unable to help ourselves because of our unlimited choice of directions, we would be equally unable to resist the myriad pressures and appeals that assail us.

The nightmare is exaggerated, but what preserves us from a version of it is the extent to which we turn away in revulsion from the prospect. We are not limitless creativity. Our transcendent finality is not a pure transcendence. We do not wholly create ourselves. Rather, we participate in and cooperate with the work of determining who we are going to be. That means that we exist in large measure within an order that is given. We are free in our response to it, but we are not free to create it. Our freedom presupposes an order beyond itself; otherwise it ceases to have any meaning. This is the paradox of human freedom. It can be exercised and preserved only within the order that has created it, sustains it, and provides its sense of direction. If we are not following the order of value disclosed within the exercise of freedom, then we are buffeted by the multiplicity of forces that beat upon us from all corners of reality. We can stand on our own only if we stand in relation to the enduring order of value glimpsed within and beyond us. We are free only to the extent that we follow a moral order.

Guidance within Freedom

What is at stake is nothing less than the gain or loss of ourselves. By holding to the movement toward higher reality we become attuned to our true selves; by dissipating ourselves in the mad pursuit of the ephemeral we slip into the abyss. Life is a deadly serious game. By freedom we can be saved or destroyed and we have no one to blame but ourselves. Despite the image of our choices as a series of discrete decisions unconnected with any larger whole, we know that the drama of our self-enactment and self-disclosure is more than that. It is the process in which we become who we are. The choices seemed so innocuously about affairs of the moment, whether to go to this place or not, to participate in this venture or that; the reality is that their real end product is ourselves. In choosing one course over another we are choosing one soul over another. We become in time one type of character rather than another. The formation of character (ethos) is very much the focus of the classical Greeks who developed our whole study of ethics. More important than the rightness or wrongness of the individual choices, their morality, they emphasized the crucial significance of becoming a certain kind of character and of the flow of choices from the nature of character.

But how should we approach that all-important struggle in which we are lost or saved? The question is no small matter in light of the transcendent freedom we possess. In contemporary parlance we are described as choosing our values, of autonomously determining our lives, of deciding the kind of person we are going to be. How can we be guided in this process when all guidance must itself be chosen by us? There is no point prior to the decision to follow one principle rather than another; otherwise it would be that predisposition that determines us and we would not really be free. No matter how much we might like to eliminate or mitigate the burden by throwing ourselves on some source of instruction as absolute, nothing can obliterate the consciousness that that too has been chosen by us. This is the appeal of all authoritarian systems and fundamentalist faiths. They provide reassurance against the uncertainty of personal decision. But they cannot abolish it.

If there is a solution to this problem it must be found within the nature of freedom itself, not by attempting to overleap it. A meditative expansion of the elementary intimations is the only means of reaching a knowledge derived from something more than caprice. It must be rooted in the very structure of freedom itself if it is to be of any use in structuring the unfolding of freedom. The most obvious place to begin is with this question of direction itself. We are in search of the truth about the moral order and informed by the sense of what is at stake in the answer. Prior to all searching there is already a sense of truth. This is not in the sense of any articulate content but in the sense that there is such a thing as truth, that is, truth in the full existential sense. We may ourselves ultimately become false or true. This is no superficial notion of the truth value attaching to propositions. It is the sense of the full significance of our life. Initially that may seem a rather modest beginning, but the conviction of the seriousness of the quest, that there is a truth and that it is worth searching for, is of inestimable value. It lifts us straightaway out of all the problems of relativism, subjectivity, and pluralism that rob the moral life of its seriousness.

But it is no more than a beginning, however indispensable it may be. The validation of the conviction is only possible by unfolding it into the discovery of truth. We must be able to cash the promissory note if it is to have any value. The crucial step occurs in the realization that this cannot be done for us. No proxy can undertake the collection of the knowledge by which we are to live. Why? Because any substitution would involve the transfer of our freedom to that other person. This may eventually be a legitimate exercise of our freedom, but it is the end rather than the beginning of the process. The first step must always be taken alone. Even if we decide to follow the guidance of another individual, a community, or a tradition, we cannot escape the structure of freedom itself. The undetermined character of our choices means that they cannot be presented to us ready-made, with their principles validated and present as a whole. All that is available to us are the most elementary intimations of truth.

Such is the nature of our freedom. It is undetermined in the sense that nothing is there prior to our decision that can compel the outcome. Nor is it utterly destitute of all assistance. But the intimations are no more than that. They are not of the order that can massively direct the unfolding of our freedom. We are free to disregard them. Not that that will make them go away, no more than following them will relieve us of the burden of decision. Fundamentally we are free because even the knowledge of order by which we are to be guided is not prior to our freedom. It is there inchoately present within that freedom, making itself felt as an inexorable undertow in the direction of goodness, but never preempting the direction we will follow. What, then, is the status of such implicit intimations? At what point can they be made the focus of explication and examination? Again, it is only through the unfolding of freedom that they can be known.

The structure of freedom is such that the principles that determine it can be known only through the responsive obedience to them. We cannot know ethical truth in the abstract or at second-hand. Or, rather, we can have a limitless supply of such generalities but they do not lead us toward any concrete action. Their usefulness might even be reduced to the function of disguising the real intention of what we do. Hypocrisy is well known as the complement that vice pays to virtue, and its instrument is the language of morality. But that is hardly knowledge of what is right. It is just enough knowledge to know what we ought to conceal but not enough knowledge to persuade us to do what is right. The interplay between freedom and knowledge within the human soul is a subtle and complex process, admitting of a wide range of amplification or suppression without reaching a limit in either direction. No matter how much we may seek to ignore the inexorable call of the good, we cannot entirely eliminate it from our consciousness. Nor is it possible to render its appeal with such force that we lose the capacity of our freedom to reject it. We have neither an absolute choice nor an absolute nonchoice. Our freedom is a drama enacted between the poles of certainty and uncertainty.

The only means of entering into the knowledge by which it is to be actualized is to set out on the path indicated before us. We may make many mistakes and missteps along the way, but even the criteria by which we discern them will only become available to us as we proceed. Only the bare minimum is present in the beginning. The barest hints and intimations that set us on the journey seem so modest and unpromising, yet they are the indispensable starting point whose depth will disclose itself more fully to us as we yield more and more to the promptings that reach us. There is no absolute beginning no more than any absolute moral knowledge. Nor would such be of much use to us. How would we recognize which absolute to follow? Which is truly absolute and how would we know? The only measure available to us is the elementary moral knowledge with which we begin our quest for the good. We can neither get back to any beginning before it nor recognize any beginning except in terms of it. The moral life consists therefore of the testing of such intimations in practice and the sifting of all instruction we receive in the diurnal struggle to follow where truth leads us.

Learning through Practice

The drama in which our lives are enacted is already going on before we become aware of our self-direction. It is part of a larger whole, and the promptings of that wider reality stream into us. They do not determine our response. We are free to accept or ignore their suggestions. But we cannot abolish their authority, nor can we escape the necessity of exercising our freedom. The intimations from beyond ourselves serve the primary function of alerting us to the character of the drama in which we find ourselves. As parts of the whole we are called to play our part in the whole and in that enterprise either preserve or destroy ourselves in the process. This is what makes the exercise of our freedom its high calling. It is the means by which we are linked to what governs the whole and participate in the same mode of intelligent self-government. We are not self-contained monads utterly free to live within their self-enclosure. Our freedom is all about openness, and its dimensions reach into mysterious regions we can barely intuit. We sense the significance of our freedom without fully comprehending it, and in that incompleteness lies the whole guarantee of its integrity.

The mystery is how the vague promptings that reach us concerning the moral order can be of much assistance in illuminating the direction we should follow. Is this all that the moral law amounts to, the barest hints that can neither be suppressed nor elaborated? How is this to provide a common moral framework for human life? The answer lies, as has long been recognized, not in the realm of theory but in that of practice. One of the most striking deficiencies in all moral theories has been the paucity of information they give about actual moral decisions. No matter what the rule or principle purported to guide us, the crucial question is always how the directives should be applied. There is never any regulation to explain how and when and to what extent we are to follow the regulation. Like recipes, they tell us everything except what we really need to know: How can I make the dish a success? On closer examination the regulative commands of various theoretical moralities turn out to be no more than abbreviations of the intimations we already possessed when we began the search. Those were the intuitions of a moral order independent of us that had prompted the quest for attunement. Are we then compelled to flounder around in a fog of moral uncertainty knowing just enough to unsettle but not enough to settle us?

The answer is, of course, that Kafkaesque anxiety does not characterize the moral life. By following its promptings we do not immerse ourselves in ever darker layers of consciousness. On the contrary, we seem to move toward luminosity. What had seemed so dimly illuminated at the beginning, for example, what fairness means in treating someone else, becomes gradually clearer to us as we seek to realize the goal more completely. Not only do the factual details of the situation, the myriad elements that must be balanced together, come into view, but we seem to acquire a firmer grasp of the moral principle involved. It ceases to be an abstraction and becomes a reality whose powerful attraction draws us onward. This in turn heightens our sensitivity to the dimensions of the situation. Aspects we had previously overlooked come into focus and we move toward a more comprehensive evaluation of the concrete challenge involved. Most striking of all is the extent to which we acquire a deeper sense of the measure that applies. We sense it no longer as an invitation from afar, glimpsed on the horizon of our consciousness. Now it emerges within us as the most *real* reality there is, as the true measure, loss of which would be loss of all that makes life meaningful. At stake is nothing less than reality itself. By responding to the pull of the moral reality that draws us, its presence is manifested more completely in our lives. The miracle of illumination occurs.

The mystery of the relationship between our freedom and the knowledge that structures and directs it is that the latter emerges only to the extent that it is actualized. The more we respond to the glimmerings that at first attract us faintly, the more they become beacons of light irradiating the path before us with unanticipated intensity. A reality that had previously seemed to offer us unlimited choice now works to constrain us within its imperious demands. Not that we ever lose the capacity to turn our backs on the higher life that calls us. But the more we respond in fidelity to its appeal, the less attractive the option of closure appears to us. We have been "captured" by the strength of that higher reality.

The option of turning aside is always there, but why would we want to exercise it when it means the loss of the only reality that counts? A human soul grows to the point that it begins to measure itself and all that it does in light of the truth of that higher reality. Rejection can still occur, but what can pull us back to a life of falsehood and meanness? The attraction of virtue and the emptiness of vice have become unmistakably clear, to the point that we might even say we have "no choice."

The knowledge this entails is hardly a matter of acquiring more information. What has changed is not that we know more about any aspects of the world or ourselves. Development has largely occurred within ourselves, in the way we view the world and the measure we apply to it. It is a growth in our "heart-knowledge," an expansiveness that puts us in touch with a scale of measurement we perceive as definitive. We have the sense of living at a higher level of reality, in comparison with which all other life is a mere dissipation of ourselves. Now we are in touch with what endures. This is the way to save ourselves, or our true selves, even if it were to mean the loss of our material well-being or even our lives. It is that discovery of an eternal scale of measurement that casts its light over the concrete situations confronting us. As we follow it even more dimensions of our duty, of what we ought to do, are illumined before us. What had hitherto been merely a vague presentiment of direction is filled with a clear understanding of the path we are obligated to pursue. The reason why knowledge of moral principles provides us neither with detailed information nor with the requisite motivation to act upon such information now becomes clear. Moral knowledge is inherently concrete knowledge. It emerges only to the extent that we participate in following it.

Gift of Love

The most mysterious point within this entire existential process is surely the beginning. What is it that draws us into the arduous challenge of fidelity to those inchoate moral intuitions before their inner appeal has become clear? By extension, we can also ask, What is it that maintains fidelity to the strain of following the upward way when we begin again to hear the siren call of relaxed abandonment to our own pleasure? This was a subject that greatly aroused the interest of Aristotle without ever resolving itself into coherence. It remained a puzzle to him why some people responded and others did not. Nor could he see what we could do to bring it about that a particular person might follow the call of virtue. Have we understood the mystery any better after two thousand years? It is difficult to say that we have, even though it remains the most crucial determinant of moral and political order. Without a sufficient number of people within any society who are imbued with a sense of unselfish nobility how can there be sufficient resistance to the forces of corruption? Beneath all problems of constitutional and social order lies this question.

Aristotle did not dwell extensively on it, assuming that it was largely a mystery inaccessible to philosophical reflection. He contented himself with the observation that nobility of soul is a gift. About its beginning little more could be said. Once a person had begun to respond to it then we could discuss the formation of virtue as a process with a definite structure. But why some people had it and others did not, why some responded and others did not, could not be penetrated.

Christianity went further than Aristotle in illumining the depth of the mystery through its reflection on the interaction of grace and freedom. The emphasis in Christianity on the divine intervention to redeem man brought to light the extent to which the human movement toward goodness always entailed a divine initiative. What Aristotle referred to as a gift of nature, coming from we know not where, Christians differentiated more clearly as the presence of divine grace. Human freedom was not eliminated—in many ways it is actually sharpened in the Christian conception—but now its dependence on an invitation beyond itself comes equally clearly into view. The mystery is deepened rather than eliminated.

Where previously it had been the mystery of the variability of gift and response, now it has been intensified as the mystery of the interaction of human freedom and divine grace. The clarity has been gained in the depth acquired, rather than in its abolition. Freedom and grace become the irreducible poles between which the drama of self-actualization or self-destruction is unfolded. Grace does not abolish freedom. No matter how strong the attraction it exercises on the human soul, we never reach the point of losing control or responsibility for the outcome. Human beings cannot hand over responsibility for who they are to become—even to God. Equally, the movement of freedom is never simply autonomous. It moves in response to what draws it, whether the source is natural or supernatural. Freedom remains mysteriously dependent on the fortuitous presence of forces that draw it beyond all that it presently is. We can never claim complete responsibility for ourselves. There is always the unattributed beginning we cannot claim as our own. None of us are self-sufficient, although we cannot turn ourselves over to anyone else. The mystery of the interaction of grace and freedom approaches the limits of what can be said about a human being.

Unintelligibility of Evil

It also brings to light a dimension of the drama that is more central than even the Greeks fully recognized. That is the mystery of evil. Nothing is more evident than the failure of self- transcendence, the refusal of the invitation to follow the attraction of virtue. We choose to remain locked within the contracted sphere of our own ego. Thinking we can dominate the world by forcing it to conform to our impulses, we resolve to reject the appeal that reaches from beyond ourselves. The Greeks understood the phenomenon of the failure of the life of virtue. Not all, not even a majority, could be counted on to follow the higher way of the opening of the soul; for most men it would only come as a result of compulsion, the purpose intended by the force of laws. The classical thinkers did not dwell on the "why" of this experience. They merely took it as a constant of the distribution of human types that defined the parameters of political order. The challenge for Plato and Aristotle was how to create a political order when only a minority of human beings are capable of achieving true inner order; the rest would have to receive their order indirectly through the force of legislation. Clearly that distribution of human character has not changed significantly. We still confront the problem of sustaining political order within a morally stratified social setting. But now we are more conscious of the intractable nature of the problem and of the extent to which its true dimensions escape us.

This is the effect of our more differentiated awareness of the inner dynamics of appeal and response, grace and freedom, than was prevalent in Greek ethics. The failure to follow the attraction of the good is not simply a random eventuality, worthy of no further examination than the distribution of natural talents. It is a failure of the person. In the most crucial decision of our lives, not about what we are to do, to use, to possess, or to enjoy, but in who we are to be, *we choose to become evil*. Plato observes the paradoxical character of this option, that a man deliberately chooses to injure himself, but he does not quite plumb the depth of darkness it contains. He limits himself to observing that such men evidently do not "see" the harm that they do to themselves, only the pain that it will cost them to make themselves better. But surely the problem is that even when they do see, or strongly intuit, the direction in which their own true good lies, they nevertheless refuse to follow it. Plato's own dialogues are frequently such efforts to open the eyes of the blind, to soften the hard-hearted, yet they are singularly unsuccessful in bringing that about through failure of persuasion. Winning the argument and piercing the shell are not sufficient. The dialogues depict although they do not dwell on·the deepest layer of the problem. Men generally know what they should do; they simply refuse to do it.

There is no explanation for this phenomenon. Mythic accounts of a flaw in the cosmos are merely a way of admitting the same thing: they render the unintelligible somewhat more manageable. They do not render it intelligible, for that is the problem of evil. It has no cause; therefore it cannot be explained. The deliberate choice of darkness and self-destruction, in the face of the appeal toward light and self-actualization, knowing full well the futility of the choice as incapable of changing the outcome, is a radical unintelligibility. There is no sufficient explanation. Without even the prospect of tangible rewards evil exercises the fascination of the limit. It draws us to taste it simply because it is forbidden. The exhilaration of going beyond all boundaries for no other purpose than that they are the confines marked out for us is the glamour of evil. Knowledge of self-destruction is not enough to restrain the soul that has resolved to reign within the hell of its own construction. Differentiation of the grace that draws and saves us heightens the radical unintelligibility of its refusal.

At the same time this differentiation discloses the precarious character of our exercise of freedom. Even the conscientious development of the habits of a lifetime, in which the practice of virtue becomes second nature, cannot remove us from the risk of yielding to the temptation of self-will. It might even generate new temptations such as the arrogance of pride. The degree of moral progress we have made might suggest the attainment of haughty self-sufficiency. Grace is no longer needed for someone of such exalted perfection. Our freedom has enabled us to overleap the struggle with weakness and temptation that is the lot of common humanity. The final temptation is, of course, to do the right thing for the wrong reason. No matter how much virtue has expanded within our souls, we never succeed in eradicating that last corner of darkness capable of harboring pride. In an unguarded moment its infection can sweep through the discipline of a lifetime. So long as we remain human beings we cannot claim to have reached the castle of perfection that seems to beckon to all of us, unless we want to demonstrate that we are of all the furthest away from it.

Tension Inescapable

The tension between good and evil in which the drama of our freedom is enacted is inescapable. Differentiation of the movement of grace that draws us toward more eminent reality does not enable us to jump out of this one. No matter how strong the pull, or our responsive pursuit of its attraction, we never succeed in breaking free from the struggle within which we are immersed. There is no point where our vigilance can be permanently relaxed. The sense of movement toward and being drawn by transcendent reality has the paradoxical effect of making us even more aware of the extent to which we are incapable of definitively breaking the bonds with this world. By giving ourselves more completely to the struggle to realize the good, we become more conscious of the degree to which we fall short. Becoming aware of the dynamics of grace and freedom, we also become aware of the extent to which the exercise of our freedom fails to reach the goal that inspires it. Faults and imperfections of which we had barely been conscious before now loom before us in all their ugliness. In the light that draws we see more clearly the infinite distance we still must cover.

The mystery of why we must thus struggle ceaselessly toward perfection arises before us. We become conscious of the strangeness of the situation in which we find ourselves. Why is it necessary for us to strain and to work in order to obtain anything? Why is it not possible for us to skip over the endless toil and find that door opening into the lost kingdom? What would be so wrong with surrendering to the relaxation of paradise? For millennia such visions have taunted humanity as it engages in its daily efforts at self-actualization. Why can it not come easier? Or if not easier, why cannot it not be attained once and for all? Why above all is the discovery of direction only available to the degree to which we have submitted ourselves to the task of following it? Why is there no one to whom we can turn over the responsibility of our lives?

The last question points us toward the only answer available to us. Even if we could entrust ourselves to the guidance of an authority, we have no way of identifying it except the inchoate moral intimations with which we begin. The unfolding of those elementary intuitions remains irrevocably our responsibility. All we can say as to why the structure is such is that it is the only way in which we can attain the full human stature of our freedom. Any other solution we can imagine involves a lessening of that most precious core. Without struggle, without the necessity of self-responsibility, without the realization of our nature through the unending quest to unfold the intimations within us, we would not be free. Without freedom we would not attain the kind of existence that is more exalted than anything else in creation. Without freedom we would not be one with the highest reality there is. Freedom is the source of our dignity.

That does not render every aspect of the mystery transparent but it does illuminate a central axis of meaning. It assures us that the mystery in which the struggle for moral knowledge and actualization, the life of virtue, is shrouded has much to do with the preservation of the transcendent finality of our freedom. Only beings who are free are capable of living the life of rationally chosen virtue, and only beings whose quest for virtue is endless could participate in a life beyond all limits. If it were possible to receive our order ready-made, then we might certainly live with more stability, but we would lose the possibility of reaching the highest reality of self-chosen order. Without risking the abyss, we could never scale the summit. Successful navigation of the dangers and rewards in the unfolding odyssey of freedom hinges on the acceptance of the parameters of mystery that guard it.

We cannot penetrate to why the rules of the game are as they are, only to the assurance that they are the means by which all that is worth gaining are to be obtained. For this reason we cannot understand why what is good is good, or why what is evil is evil. Ultimate knowledge of good and evil is denied man. All that we can know is the difference between good and evil. The necessity of following one and avoiding the other is given to us through the intimations with which we begin. We cannot reach behind that beginning to any comprehension of their necessity. The attempt to do so does not result in grasping anything. We end by losing even the limited knowledge available to us as, imagining we have become like gods, we no longer even have the human knowledge of the difference between good and evil. Having assumed we had dispensed with those elementary landmarks we now have even less to guide us. The result is clearly the fall from paradise.

Only by holding firmly to the only intimations we have can we move toward the only good available to us. By attempting to overleap the conditions that bind us, even the intimations with which we began slip away from us. The way toward knowledge of the good remains the arduous struggle to conform our lives to it. No other avenue is provided for us. But for those who are willing to accept the conditions of the search, the concrete living out of the moral indications already there turn out to yield a harvest of understanding beyond our expectations. The constant surprise is the discovery that our moral knowledge is not fixed, but instead capable of a dynamic unfolding in response to our participation within it. We cannot reach back behind the moral knowledge already there when we begin, nor can we jump forward to its final denouement beyond ourselves. Yet if we are content to explore within the limits of our existential participation we discover an unexpected expansion of meaning. The dynamic enlargement of what we know is only available if we accept the mystery of its limits.

Growth of Soul

That is the route not only toward knowledge, but toward the only higher life available to us. We may not know whence it comes or whither it draws us, but while we respond to the undeniable moral stirrings within us we sense the reality toward which they direct us. Beyond knowledge they draw us toward the most real reality there is. It can be approached only through the mystery of participation within its ordering rule. Any attempt to take possession of its strength by force yields nothing but an empty fist and the dizzying descent of those who have lost their only foothold on the reality that endures. But so long as we respond to its pull upon us, it draws us up toward the higher life we sensed from the beginning. We see that human life is not primarily about following a moral code or measuring up to some abstract principles. They are only the outer markings for the inner reality of the growth of the soul.

This is the core of the moral life. It is the great discovery reached through the existential struggle to live in fidelity to the moral order. What had previously appeared a daunting, if not impossible, task, suddenly reveals itself as self-sustaining and easy. The painful exertion of discipline that had dominated our perspective at the start melts away, to disclose the inner expansive joyfulness as the secret of its life. It is not that exertion disappears, only that now it is experienced as an exhilarating enlargement of the heart. Progressively we are drawn beyond the boundaries of self-giving we had always accepted as fixed into a realm brighter and broader than anything hitherto experienced. We discover reserves of nobility within ourselves we had never thought possible and barely even suspected. The call to perfection is limitless and, however far we still have to go, the distance we have already traveled has exceeded all our expectations. In becoming better than we thought we could be we discover the self-justifying movement of the moral life.

Of course, the information yielded by this existential discovery is limited. We have no further comprehension of why our experience is structured in this way, why we must move from narrow self-contraction to an expansive enlargement of our capacities, nor how or when the mysterious process will reach its fulfillment, nor even whether we will be able to persevere with fidelity on the higher course we contemplate before us. We are still surrounded by mystery. The difference is that now it is pierced more strongly by the light that had never entirely disappeared but whose dimness we were inclined to confuse with the mystery itself. We do not need any information about the source of the process, its necessity, or its consummation. We have firsthand acquaintance with the movement toward the life it entails so long as we respond to the promptings placed before us. We know it is good. Further explanation as to how and why would be superfluous since they would add nothing to the central reality of the movement toward fuller reality we experience within us. In our most visionary moments we recognize that such knowledge might even constitute an obstacle. The unfolding of our free response of love depends on our choosing in light of the invitation of love without any other considerations.

Knowledge of where and how and why we are moving would add nothing to the essence. Rather, it would jeopardize the purity of the response since it would introduce an element of detachment, inviting reflection on our place in the overall process. By drawing us away from the immediate focus on our obligations, it would dissipate our attention in the peripheral. It might even tempt us to place ourselves at the center of the universe. By seeing through everything we would end by seeing nothing. Without an existential movement and horizon that is given we would lose all constant points of reference. Thinking we had gained knowledge and freedom, we would discover we had neither. Nothing would any longer mean anything to us, since everything would be the same and all equally transparent. Without a goal that draws us we would be incapable of movement, for nothing could be a source of attraction for us. The only movement possible would be the random fluttering of leaves that blow with every passing breeze. We would quickly discover that knowledge and freedom no longer hold any meaning for us. Gladly we would return to the horizon of mystery that formerly structured and made possible the joyous movement of discovery by which we exercised our free self-responsibility.

Fortunately, there is little danger of such an illusory escape since it cannot be effected through our dreaming about it. But the unhindered exercise of our freedom is dependent on exorcising the appeal of the illusion. We must recognize it as one of the perennial temptations capable of assuming many guises and unlikely to be absent from consciousness for long. The disappearance of one form of it, such as the belief in the possibility of a global system of explanation, is very often replaced by another, such as despair at the possibility of discovering any meaning. We have witnessed this transition in our own time. The last of the militant global ideologies, communism, collapsed intellectually with the fall of the Berlin Wall. It no longer has any credibility as a systematic account of human history, and all successor claimants have become exhausted. We are now in an age of more widespread despair at the possibility of discovering any coherence. It is a view embraced with a variety of tonalities, whether exultantly by the deconstructionists or dejectedly by their conservative opponents. Relativism and the attendant vacillations between fundamentalism and nihilism are all that remain. It is the same apocalyptic mind-set that will have either everything explained or nothing that is at work. The unwillingness to accept the partial knowledge available to human beings is still the problem. Most crucial in overcoming the opposition is to recognize that that limited perspective that is ours is no incidental viewpoint. It is not a random slice of information but a knowledge of the most central mystery there is. It is a heart-knowledge of the love that sustains all. But the only avenue we have to it lies through the acceptance of the darkness in which it is enclosed in order to draw us freely and fully into its embrace.

The task of establishing the only authoritative meaning available to us is, moreover, not so insuperable as it appears. Despite the pervasive impression that we float on a sea of relativism and that the best we can do is cobble together whatever fragments of meaning come our way, this does not change the abiding intimations of the human condition. We are still anchored by the permanent forces that draw us even if we no longer know that they hold us fast. Even the denial that we possess any universal moral knowledge cannot eradicate the elementary sense of right and wrong from our hearts. It remains unobtrusively present, awaiting the time when the strength of the crisis we confront evokes articulate awareness of its force. Knowledge of the moral order beyond us can remain routine, confused with convention and civility, until the moment when a movement of resistance to what we are pressed to accept rises within us. Then it becomes unmistakably clear that we do not make our own rules. We must decide for or against what is truly evil and either become such or save ourselves from its deadly influence. When our choice is thus narrowed to the essentials we recognize the truth of the knowledge that guides us.

It is the same prearticulate knowledge that enables us to recognize the authoritative truth in the statements and actions of others. What makes it possible for human beings to form a community includes language, bonds of sympathy, mutual necessity, and so on. But its most essential ingredient is the capacity to recognize a common moral order. That is what creates the authority of public truth. It is not something imposed, for then it would not create a common world of meaning. The imposition of order by one individual on others does not create a community. Only if they are capable of seeing the same things from the same point of view do they live in the same common world. Then they can share a common good and possess the means of ordering their efforts toward it. Nothing is more indispensable to this than the existence of a common sense of the fairness or justice of their mutual arrangements. That cannot be created. It can be evoked but only because it already preexists in the common moral knowledge inchoately present within each of us. It is on that basis that we can recognize the rightness of what is proposed.

There is no going back to a beginning prior to the beginning. We find ourselves in possession of some undeveloped moral intuitions, and from there we can begin to reflect and discuss. We cannot presuppose nothing or assume that we might be able to begin from zero. Even the question of what is right or wrong presupposes some sense of what we mean and of what will decide the issue. We are in search of that which is good or just independent of our personal wishes or inclinations, and we are guided in the search by the sense of what that goal is. We will recognize it when we reach it because we already know it in germ. Otherwise we would not even have begun the search for it. The key, as we have noted, is to begin the exploration in an existential mode, not under the illusion that we might be able to reach our goal as detached observers from the outside. The moral order of which we seek fuller knowledge will only disclose itself to those who seek to order their lives in accordance with it. Ethics, as Aristotle observed, is a practical science and its truth is more fully disclosed in concrete action than in the universal principles.

In the midst of the philosophical confusion and moral disorientation that surrounds contemporary discussion, the only advice is to take the first step in the direction of what we sense to be good. Just do it. Where we begin is not so important as that we make a beginning. Gradually the direction we should follow will reveal itself more fully, and as we pursue it more faithfully its further extension and power will emerge before us. The bedeviling problem of relativism, of the ineradicable pluralism of our moral universe, begins to recede in significance. By undertaking the concrete effort of resistance to the bad and attunement to the good we enter into the real moral order, and in it we encounter those who have similarly submitted themselves to its fateful authority. "Live not by lies" was the powerful advice given by Solzhenitsyn to his countrymen in a time of massive totalitarian deception. It does not matter where you draw the line between truth and the lie, he explained. Simply begin where you perceive it. By refusing to go along with the lie the area of truth will be gradually expanded, eventually revealing itself as the measure by which we are to be judged.

In that light the paltriness and mendacity of all our machinations about the loss of an objective moral order stand exposed. They appear as suspiciously hollow complaints designed to relieve us of the burden of existential struggle. Or it is a counsel of despair that seems ultimately to serve the same purpose. The prospect of dislodging such pervasive suspicion of morality must be based on the self-awareness of the limited application of the approach. We cannot suspect everything without suspecting our suspicion itself. Why should we even be concerned about the groundlessness of moral convictions if we did not sense that they should be built upon a rock of certainty? That hunger for what endures is the impulse that guides us, but it must not be allowed to derail into a premature grasp of whatever carries the appearance of solidity. Only the real thing will do, and this real thing must be sought in the only arena where it is to be found. The truth can only emerge in living life. We must take up the daily struggle, persevering in it without seeking to short-circuit the process of moral growth. The only thing capable of breaking the spell of false absolutes and the charm of absolute despair is the expansive power of reality itself.

The appeal of illusion is dispelled through the recognition that the only route toward the higher life available to us lies in accepting the conditions of the struggle. The counterfeit may have a certain easy attraction but it cannot stand before the real thing. Once we recognize that the only meaning and certainty available to us is the truth that emerges within us when we give ourselves to its guidance, there will be no need to look for any alternatives. The tangible movement toward that higher reality drawing us is sufficient justification. All other proof would be both superfluous and unreal. It still may not yield conclusive explanation as to why what is good is good, or what is bad is bad. We still may reach a stopping point in our quest for justifications. The mystery of good and evil has not been breached. But we have acquired a firm grasp on the only meaning and assurance that is available to us. We know that the pursuit of the good draws us toward the higher life, touching on what is immortal and forever. It is the way that saves us from dissolution into the multiplicity of forces impinging upon us, an endless waste without even the touch of any higher meaning.

The difficulty in setting out on such a journey whose end is not so clearly known in advance is always the beginning. What can reassure us that the quest will yield that of which we are in search? Or is it possible, as Descartes hypothesized, that we might be the victims of some cruel hoax played by a cosmic trickster?

What indeed can sustain us when the going gets tough and we are inclined to despair of ever reaching or moving toward our goal? Again, there must be another dimension to the moral life whose presence we depended upon but have not yet brought to our attention. This is the dimension of faith. From the very beginning there must be some sense of assurance of the validity of our struggle. We must possess the sense that it is not in vain, doomed from the start to end in futility or failure. We had earlier talked about the process as one of being drawn from sources beyond ourselves, of the dimension of grace that pulls and lifts us beyond the limits of what we ever thought possible. The gift of love enlarging our hearts is surely the beginning. Now we must reflect on the faith in which it is contained and whose articulation is essential to the meaningful order that sustains us. We are not alone, and we cannot undertake the odyssey of the soul in fragile and uncertain isolation. The moral life cannot avoid the recognition that its boundary is guarded by the inescapable mystery of God.

CHAPTER 4

THE MYSTERY OF GOD

T HE GREAT difficulty in the odyssey of self-enactment and self-disclosure of human freedom is the faith that sustains the voyage. What is there to prevent us from giving up prematurely along the way? Obstacles and stumbling blocks occur with depressing regularity. How do we know they are not indicators of our permanent incapacity to reach our goal? Perhaps human life is one absurd struggle against impossible odds to reach an unattainable end. Is our experience not one long frustration and failure? Besides, everything we know has an end. What possible significance can our actions carry when we have reached the physical limits of our life? Disappointment and death finally put their seal on even our most grandiose aspirations, mocking definitively the modest progress we might have managed to win before we go into the "last good night." How can we hold off the conclusion that human life is "a tale told by an idiot, full of sound and fury, signifying nothing?"

It is not enough to be touched by the attraction of a higher meaning. Something more is needed than the aspiration toward goodness. There must be some assurance that the goal is real, that it is attainable even if we as struggling individuals seem incapable of reaching it, and that our part is to remain faithful to a quest whose mysterious depth is impenetrable from the perspective of participation. Before we can set out, we must possess a knowledge of our goal through faith. Even more, if we are to persevere in the face of the evident discouragement and disappointment that comes our way, we must have an underlying certainty that preserves us from wavering from our course. Otherwise our inspiration will prove as insubstantial as the seed that fell on bad ground: without roots it was unable to withstand the difficulties that predictably assailed it. Only if the guiding intimations of our heart are linked to the higher reality itself will they be able to withstand the denigrating pressures that assail it. Without faith we will not be able to maintain the truth of our innermost convictions in the face of their dismissal by the evident callousness of life. Faith is our lifeline to the invisible reality that draws us.

But where does faith come from and what is the secret of its power? Faith is not the same as optimism, the unfounded generalized confidence that everything will work out well. Such an attitude is very often confused with faith but in reality they are poles apart. Optimism is a plaintive shadow of faith, the proverbial straw grasped at when all sense of the source of faith has slipped away. In contrast, the essence of faith is the presence of that which is the goal revealed within it. Faith is not an empty bet on the future. It is the knowledge of that toward which we are striving now held firmly in light of the presence that reveals itself as our goal. Metaphors of blindness and a leap, contrary to the misimpression of Kierkegaard's famous reflections, are profoundly inappropriate to the reality. No blind leap is required since faith is a source of luminosity that radiates its meaning over our life the more we respond to its opening. The expanding luminosity of faith parallels and sustains the larger movement of our lives toward fuller participation in the goodness transcending all else.

Revelation

Faith is a revelation. That which draws us in pursuit of the good stands before us as the divine presence we ultimately seek. Only now we not merely hold it as an intimation, darkly glimpsed as the goal of the search, we fleetingly behold it as the presence that reveals itself to us. The horizon of mystery surrounding our existence is pierced briefly as we encounter the divine personality. We are addressed and we respond. What is said matters much less than that an exchange occurs, because no words can convey the meaning of the event in which even for a moment we are permitted to touch the divine presence. Any words entailed are purely incidental. The overwhelming significance is that we have been briefly touched by transcendent Being and we retain the unmistakable sense of the distance separating it from all else. What content can compare with that knowledge or what discourse could adequately convey it to one who had no sense of it? Words alone would be ineffective in communicating what must first be experienced in order to understand that to which they refer.

Fortunately, such experiences are not so unusual that they must be considered the preserve of a spiritual elite. They seem to be experiences that occur with considerable frequency to human beings, although they are unique in happening entirely outside of our command or control. We cannot take hold of or transfer an experience of God. Instead, he reveals himself experientially to whom he wills. And even when we feel weighed down by the routine of everyday life, we are never so far away from the border of mystery that we have lost all sense of the presence beyond. We are pulled toward participation in higher reality and we know the direction in which divine being lies. But this is not quite the same as feeling the unmistakable touch of the divine presence. That is an opening or, rather, a deepening of the mystery for which we are always unprepared. It breaks unexpectedly into our more or less organized existence, reordering everything through its own unforgettable reality. The experience occurs unpredictably but with sufficient frequency that it may be taken as an abiding dimension of our nature. Both from the direction of the moral attraction drawing us and our own occasional experiences of its divine consummation, we know what people are talking about when they describe such encounters.

We recognize the longing from which they begin. There would be no openness toward transcendent revelation if there was not already a hunger to know it. Even more, there would not be a thrusting movement toward divine being if we were not already drawn by its presence within us. What is it that makes us ache to touch the great mystery surrounding our lives? It is that we already sense it and want to arrive at a fullness of knowledge of it. Otherwise the whole drive toward transcendence is inexplicable. Nothing within this world explains it. What can so relentlessly drive us on beyond all finite achievements and satisfactions, rendering their fulfillment pitifully stale? It can only be that we are drawn by a heart-knowledge of that higher being that absolutely will not let us rest with even the most plentiful of finite goods. We are driven toward that higher, transcendent reality because we already know its touch within us. It absolutely will not rest until we rest with it. The search can end only when it arrives at the fullness of Being that it recognizes as the reality that drew us from the very beginning.

Recognition occurs because we encounter the presence we have always known. It is not as familiar and comfortable as an old shoe, but it is recognized as the enduring, constant reality at the border of our consciousness. It is that which was the substance of the horizon of mystery guarding our every moment. We know the boundary not as a mere vacuousness, but as a fullness of reality. It is not an empty expanse of space, the meaningless extent of the unknown unknown, but an intensity of higher life that casts its tantalizing meaning over everything else in existence. We are drawn toward it, not as toward an abyss, but toward an abundance beyond measure. Even when we sense it as an abyss in which we might lose ourselves, our fascination is always that it promises a release from the everyday into the transcendent. Now for a brief magical moment all that looking toward an unlimited horizon is rewarded. The mystery that seemed to guard its own secret so well inexplicably comes into partial focus. We see through to the depths of divine being it contains. That is the outburst of revelation.

Then inevitably the clouds descend again on our vision. We see no further than our own longing illuminates and we understand that that is as it should be. Revelation cannot come from us or through our efforts, however intense and well directed they may be. If it is to be a revelation of transcendent Being then it must come from beyond. How else could it be that which is different from all other reality, the goal of our dissatisfaction with all existing things? To be the answer to the thirst for what is beyond all limits, it must come from the reality that transcends the finitude of everything else in existence. How can that be known by finite beings such as ourselves? All that we know comes before us wrapped in the same finite character as ourselves. We are locked within the finite limits of our own vision. Everything we can conceive is similarly constricted. Only if the force of transcendent Being makes itself present can we have any sense of its existence. We can only know God through his self-revelation. Our nature can reach no further than the awareness of its limits. The unlimited can be glimpsed only to the extent that it makes itself manifest. Then it is embraced as the goal of our longing, ever old and ever new, as Saint Augustine described it. We recognize the transcendent divine presence for which we had lain in waiting, but we know that it can only come from that which is its own source.

Nothing can provide the sense of transcendent reality except transcendent Being itself. There can be no knowledge of it except to the extent that it reveals itself to us, for no other reality can bridge the gulf that separates everything else from it. God can only be revealed by himself. There may be many intermediaries, many intervening stages on the way, but they derive their power from that which they are not. They point toward it, but they cannot communicate it. Only that which *is* can reveal itself to us. Everything else falls short. That is why the revelation is grasped as an unmistakable truth. It is impossible for us to be deceived by it because only that which is transcendent God can impress itself as such upon us. We know all other beings as less than the highest. Therefore they cannot be that which we seek. There can be no doubt about the sense of that which is the measure of all truth because it enters into our consciousness as the fullness of all reality. Beyond it there is nothing.

Transcendent Measure of All Things

The paradox is that having touched on that which is the fullness of all reality we retain nothing by way of information. Nothing has changed in the aggregate of things within our experience. We have neither superior insight nor superior power as a consequence. Everything is as it was before, yet everything is changed utterly. The encounter with that which *is* has stamped all else as transitory. We can no longer mistake any finite achievement or fulfillment for our final end. Transcendent reality has shattered the appeal of the substitute. Other than that deep confirmation of the intimations already structuring our beginning, nothing more is attained. Yet that is sufficient. A scale of measurement as immoveable as the universe is of more value than all the information in existence. What we most need is not knowledge but a means of measuring its significance. Transcendent reality is the measure because it is itself beyond all measure. All that is measured and known is already within the boundaries of the limited. The boundary reality itself cannot be bounded.

It is beyond all categories, all contents, and all possibilities of representation. The transcendent transcends all essence. That is why it cannot yield any immanent information or instructions. But because it is the ground, Being constitutes the order of everything else in existence. As human beings we are called to respond freely to its structuring influence. That which is the source of all reality reveals itself to us as the indubitable source. Our freedom itself might even be jeopardized were it not that the revelation unfolds sequentially through our responsive submission to its ordering force. Only one who is already prepared to obey the voice of God is capable of hearing its ordering command. But once heard it cannot be forgotten. Nor can it be doubted, for it manifests itself as the most real reality there is. It is the fullness of being. All our judgment of reality must take place in relation to that which is the most real. The measure cannot be measured. In comparison to it all else is of a lesser degree of reality.

Striking, however, is the contrast between the imposing divine authority of our experience and its silence within the field of human history. Why are so many deaf to the voice of God? Could it be that they do not hear him? How, then, is it impossible for us to ignore his penetrating authority within us? Most of all, how can that which impresses us as the fullness of all reality fail to reach the souls of so many others? The answer lies in the peculiarly responsive and participatory structure of spiritual experience. It is like the fulfillment of the divine promises that can only be verified by obedience to them. The authenticity of the divine voice is vouchsafed only to the extent that we submit to its direction. Grounds for belief consist in the fulfillment of its promises, and those promises will be realized only in those who move toward them in faith. It is an expanding circular movement, just as it had been from the very questions that began the meditation.

Not even the expanding radiance that draws us can destroy the inviolable freedom of our response. The consummation within the outburst of revelation is simultaneously the limit of our submission to the authority of transcendent Being.

Struggle for Recollection

Yet even that powerful illumination cannot abolish the other abiding feature of the human condition. All that we know declines, including our knowledge itself. No matter how penetrating the encounter with transcendent revelation, nothing can prevent the movement away from consciousness of its profound reality. When the momentary glimpse has passed forgetfulness sets in. Gradually the memory fades and slowly its hold on us begins to weaken. Soon it is barely a memory and it is only with difficulty that we can hold onto its authoritative truth. The press of more immediate concerns—physical, emotional, and material—invades our consciousness and we begin to wonder whether anything really significant happened at all. Did we indeed dream it all up? How can we live our lives in unwavering fidelity to what was no more than a fleeting impression, a burning bush, a "voice," and at bottom just a sense of presence? How can this be the substantial reality when we are daily confronted with the necessities of existence? Surely the material and massively emotional demands of our lives are the reality. How can we measure them in relation to a glimpse of transcendence no sooner grasped than it is gone? Having come down from the magical opening on the mountain we must confront anew the inescapable struggle for survival within this world.

Memory seems a slender thread on which to preserve and conserve the revelation bestowed on us in that moment. Indeed, it is impossible for us as humans to retain anything as a pure memory. As embodied spirits we require our spirituality to be expressed if it is to be retained at all. Perhaps one of the great problems of our secular age, if not its defining feature, is that the episodic life of the spirit slips away without any chance of encapsulation. Nothing can be retained if there is no suitable means of symbolization available. Even the most mystical illuminations can hardly have a continuity if they encounter only an atmosphere of dismissal and suspicion. How can you be a mystic if you are immediately regarded as mentally imbalanced? Even the force of transcendent truth could not withstand that disdain, without violently altering the conditions of human life. Short of an apocalyptic divine intervention, the continuity of spiritual experience can be guaranteed through the only means hitherto available within history. Revelatory experience must reach symbolization in order to endure.

Only then does it stand a chance of persisting amid the vacillating states of consciousness through which a human being passes. Depiction of the reality beyond all seeing does not render it visible in the solid manner in which trees and cars and dogs enter our awareness. But it does give the momentary glimpses, in which the overwhelming truth of that reality comes into our consciousness, a greater permanency. They are less easily dismissed or forgotten. We are reminded more substantively of them even when we feel far away from the state in which we beheld its presence. Most importantly, the objectivity of symbols within the social world has a mutually reinforcing effect. That which is regarded by all others we know as a reality has a much more sturdy character to it than that which we contemplate only in the uncertain privacy of our own hearts. We mutually reassure and are reassured that the mysterious presence gently but powerfully drawing us was no private illusion. It now exists as a common, publicly authoritative truth. The stability thus imparted to the glimpses of transcendent Being is not the source of subsequent experiences, nor is it sufficient to keep them alive. But it does extend the memory of the revelatory eruptions and it does provide the conditions in which an openness to their recurrence is evoked. The spirit, of course, continues to blow where it will.

The difference is that now it blows in and around a historically existing symbolic tradition. This is what is conventionally referred to as "revelation." The term is ascribed to the spiritual traditions most decisively claiming to have originated in divine inspiration. But on closer examination all spiritual traditions as far as we can trace them begin in a hierophany, a revelation of the sacred. The theophanies of the revealed religions, Judaism, Christianity, and Islam, are no more than a special case of the divine origination of all faith. They are distinguished not through their monotheism, which is a possibility of wide amplification, but through the definitively transcendent character of their revelation. Only the conceit of modern rational speculation has proposed the suggestion of the human origin of religion. The ancient world understood the human contribution to the depiction of the gods, but it understood that their authorization could only come from the divine side. It is a superficial error, betraying a signal shallowness, to think that human beings could worship any source so readily exposed as its own construction. Nietzsche's dismissal of it as barely concealed nihilism has been enough to eliminate its credibility.

But Nietzsche has been much less successful, historically and philosophically, in exploding the traditional carriers of faith. Despite his suggestion, as the head of a long line of such deconstructionists, of their human origin, the followers of such faiths do not recognize the force of his critique. They have more tangible proof of the divine origination of the revelatory traditions. The illusion that so many of the great secular heroes confidently proclaimed as dead or without a future has proved impressively persistent at the end of the twentieth century. To find an explanation it is necessary to examine the character of the experiences behind them. Followers of the world religions persevere because they carry within themselves the fleeting but inescapable contact with the revelatory sources themselves. They do not doubt the validity of their symbolic traditions because they recognize them as the authoritative carriers of the elementary divine presence intuited directly within. The powerful inward experience directs them to its external historical articulations. They recognize themselves within the traditional religious forms. This is the secret of the persistence of ancient faiths in the midst of our contemporary secular world.

Secular Openness toward Revelation

Despite the impressive technical progress and the more modest social and political progress we enjoy, human life remains pretty much what it has always been. It is lived within the same fragile balance between life and death, guarded by the boundary of mystery we are incapable of surpassing. We may have a greater variety of distractions and escapes available to us, the inevitableness of death may seem more remote, but all that superiority is as much an illusion serving only to undermine the seriousness of our quest for meaning. Sooner or later we are forced to confront the limitations of our existence. Indeed, the awareness of imperfection is to some extent heightened by the modern achievements. Having moved so far toward fulfilling our needs we are seduced by the expectation that all our longings can be satisfied and eventually crushed by the discovery of the impossibility of the project. What, then, has the whole gigantic effort of the modern world been all about? The awakening of restlessness is one of the unintended consequences of the modern pursuit of satisfaction.

The awareness of the finitude of all achievements is reinforced by the discovery of the incapacity to fulfill our moral aspirations. Not only are our lower desires frustrated but our higher commitments are incapable of realization as well. No sooner do we recognize the moral perfection toward which we are called than we become aware of the impossible distance remaining for us to traverse. Many lifetimes would be required in order to have some chance of gaining the goal of moral perfection that seems to call us. Even the attainability of our full moral development under such conditions is not so evident. What is clear is that we are presently incapable of reaching that toward which our capacity directs us. Doomed to frustration, our lives appear even more problematic. What kind of existence is it in which we are consciously directed toward a goal of moral perfection we are incapable of attaining? The finiteness of our moral attainments is a special case of the ultimate frustration of all our desires. But it is a crucial case because it makes us conscious of the higher life we are blocked from reaching. The unlimited aspiration of our existence is no longer blind; now it is revealed as a movement toward full spiritual life.

The paradox of freedom we observed earlier can only be sustained if we can find a way of preserving the balance of meaning. Freedom requires the recognition that it is incapable of definitively reaching its goal. It is an unlimited openness, never capable of resting within its immanent satisfactions. Every goal reached is a stepping-stone to the one beyond it. Yet it cannot be permitted to view itself as an endless unfolding of futility. The fact that its end is unattainable in any limited, concrete fulfillment does not condemn it to wearing itself out in frustration. We have seen that it is the paradox of its incompleteness that preserves our freedom—but only so long as we retain some sense of its ultimate completion beyond this life. The mystery of grace that initially draws us from we know not where must be allowed to work its illuminative effect. We must be allowed to discover slowly that as the source of our movement lies not wholly within ourselves, so its final fulfillment is also warranted by the same transcendent reality that draws us. The recognition of the divine source of the attraction we experience is the turning point. That is the spark that assures us of the transcendent finality of our existence.

We recognize the validity of the historical symbolizations of our movement toward union with God after death. But we believe in them not simply because we desire the continuation of our life after death. Rather, it is that we have such an aspiration because we already experience a life that is larger than what can be contained within this one. The historic revelatory accounts are accepted not because they represent an escape from the frustrations of life in the world, they are embraced for the same reasons human beings have flocked to them for millennia. They are the most satisfactory accounts of the tensional structure of our experience here and now. Only through the movement toward transfiguration beyond the world can we give due weight to all of the dimensions that reach into us without distortion or illusion. The revelatory accounts represent in that sense the most rational articulation of the order of our existence. This is particularly in evidence when we are compelled to confront the darkest mystery of evil.

Not only does our moral life fall short of its final aspiration, but we recurrently fail to meet even our immediately attainable obligations. Failure is the constant in our moral life. It is curious to notice policymakers' inability to deal with this reality when they employ the secular terminology of social and political analysis. They speak confidently of campaigns to wipe out domestic violence, drug and alcohol abuse, and the scourges of crime and cruelty in our society. But how can these human weaknesses be removed without also removing human beings as well? As long as we have one we will have the other. Of course, much can be done to resist and oppose crime, violence, and abuse, but they will never be eliminated so long as we remain the creatures we are. How do we know this? The irrefutable proof lies within our own hearts. We know our own weakness and propensity to evil. We are capable of the most amazing callousness even toward those whom we purport to love. Neither the most vociferous protestations of our best intentions nor the sting of remorse at our failures are enough to prevent our descent into the darkness of self-assertive ego. We are inclined to say that we can't help ourselves, although we know that that too is a lie.

Evil has no explanation, which is why it has no cause. A multitude of excuses can be produced but none of them justify the wanton wickedness committed. We know it is wrong and yet we do it anyway. The defect lies not in our knowledge or in our capacity, but in our inability to avoid transgressing the line we see before us. Indeed, the very forbiddenness of the actions is often enough of an enticement, quite apart from any tangible returns we may expect to obtain by engaging in them. We may say that it is the glamour of evil that seduces us, that for the moment obscures our more clear-sighted perception of the misery it will cause to ourselves and to others. But the obscurity is never so total nor the attraction so fatal that we cannot resist. If it were, then we would no longer be free and the action would no longer be evil. The fall into nonbeing is one of the possibilities contained in beings whose free choice is ultimately what determines their nature. Freedom always contains the option of turning away from being. We can choose to destroy ourselves. That is the unintelligibility, the heart of darkness, that recurrently draws us over the edge. The great danger is that we will not be able to make our way back if the pull of life has weakened to the point that we no longer perceive its call.

The struggle between good and evil reaches a new level of intensity in the realization that even our freedom is in jeopardy. We may have freely chosen to wander off the path of virtue, but having become more vicious we are now relatively powerless to change our character. The grip of evil can become stronger the more we yield to its blandishments. One day we awaken to discover that even if we will to change we would not be so capable. The relative fixity of character was recognized by the classical philosophers who understood it as the product of practice. Who we are is not determined in disconnected episodes. Rather, the formation of character is the effect of habit produced by a lifetime of actions of a particular type. What was less closely examined by Aristotle is the iron necessity of habit which cannot so easily be broken. How can we take even the first step toward a goal that has lost all attraction for us? Of course, there is no human being for whom the voice of good has become utterly silent, but it can become so faint that its motive force no longer penetrates our hardness of heart. Then the necessity for the dramatic intervention of grace, an infusion from beyond, is brought to focal awareness. When the movement of grace does break through it is recognized as the reality that saves us from our own powerlessness.

Redemptive Divine Action

As the free gift of love grace reveals itself as the ultimate redemptive force in the universe. Not only is the outpouring of transcendent grace the only means of breaking through the barrier of deafness with which our souls are surrounded. Not only is it the only means of dramatically converting character held fast by the chains it has chosen to place on itself. Not only is grace the only means of liberating our freedom. It is also the route to the definitive triumph of good over evil in the world. It is the answer to what Marx called "the riddle of history." The cycle of exploitation and oppression is broken only through the suffering endurance of the limits of human evil. Even if the appeal of grace in specific individuals goes unheard, as indeed the persistence of evil in the world makes evident, the eventual triumph of goodness is assured in suffering endurance of the limits of evil. By the outpouring of love without condition the victory of good over evil has taken place.

The conflict between the invincibility of goodness and the persistence of evil has been resolved. We know directly the power of goodness that draws us, that it is a reality superior to all other realities, that it is the life of transcendent Being itself. The revelation of God makes this abundantly clear. Nothing can withstand the presence of that highest reality. In comparison to it evil is no more than the empty glitter that distracts us, a mere puff of smoke easily blown away. But then we encounter the stubborn resistance of ourselves and our world to submission before the ordering divine will. When we are no longer standing within its light we prefer to follow our own will. The recalcitrance of human reality, its rebellion, forces us to conclude that transcendent order can only be realized through an apocalyptic transfiguration of history. From visions of the Armageddon to total revolution, the all-destroying and all-transforming divine force is an abiding symbol of our imagination. Some variant of it seems to be the only means of resolving the contradiction between the inexorable force of good and the intractable persistence of evil in our lives.

But then we notice the element of overreaching in all such speculation. It is rooted in human impatience with the condition in which we find ourselves. We do not want to endure in the uncertain conflict between good and evil in which we find ourselves. Far better to jump out of our situation into that next phase when the victory is assured and definitive. At the back of it all there is even an element of revolt in this attitude itself. There is an impatience with the perspective allowed to man. We want to vault into the viewpoint of eternity to see the whole, complete and resolved, as God does. The impatience is ultimately with merely being a man and the desire to leap into the position of God. At least from the perspective of knowledge we want to see the resolution of the conflict as God does. But that is not possible, nor does it indicate that we have yet been fully able to find ourselves on God's side of the conflict. If we were, then we would be prepared to humbly submit to the mysterious will of God. We would be content to take our place in the great cosmic drama, without murmuring. It is God's prerogative to know the day and the hour of its final resolution, just as it is in his hands to bring about the ultimate defeat of evil through the power of good.

Even the movement of our hearts in pursuit of the good is not wholly our own. We are drawn by a grace we perceive to be beyond our own nature. Beyond the capacity of our own efforts we sense that the good toward which we are ultimately moved is the good that transcends all finite existence. Much lies within our own deliberate capacity—modest progress in self-improvement and virtue can be made—but what sustains the movement as a whole is that it is directed toward a life beyond all that we have known. It is the touch of transcendent Being that calls forth our most heroic efforts, supporting and sustaining them in the face of obstacles we felt insurmountable, and providing all the incentive for the struggle as a whole. The taste of that more eminent reality is what lifts us finally beyond ourselves. We are touched by a supernatural love. At the end of it all we know that, whatever the contribution of our efforts, the power has all been from the divine side that moves us and is the source of our capacity as well.

The mystery of the struggle with evil is ultimately the mystery of the outpouring of God's grace. The struggle is ultimately between divine grace and the spirit of rebellion. Our role is to be free and conscious participants within the drama that is in part played through us, but it is not to be that of the dramatist who is in charge of writing the script. We must play our part without seeking to escape it. It is enough for us to know that the triumph of divine goodness is assured, because it is the power of reality opposing the darkness of unreality, and that there is no better way for the drama to unfold toward its transfiguring fulfillment of all things. The suffering rejection of grace is primarily God's suffering of the consequences of the free choice of evil. It is only secondarily our suffering. To the extent that we submit to the divine will, then we become participants in the divine mysterious suffering of revolt. To that extent, we join our efforts with God's mysterious work of redeeming the fallen condition of our world. The deepest insight we can attain is the recognition of the redemptive divine transfiguration already underway within history.

We cannot know why our suffering of evil can have this redemptive effect. There is no code book to the mystery of representative suffering. We only know that it is so and that even the efforts that seem to bear least fruit, so long as they are truly directed toward the good, will yield a harvest of transformation. In this sense we are parts of a connected whole. If we add to the sum total of good in the universe, then we will have moved the scales in that direction; if we indulge in revolt, then we will have shifted things in the opposite way. The reason is that we know the struggle between good and evil within us as part of a divine cosmic conflict. Its truth is that goodness overcomes evil through the power of love and, even if the triumph is not apparent in any particular episode, the reality of one and the unreality of the other is irrefutable. We sense directly the incomparable distance between them. Even in defeat the incomparable power of love is revealed. It is the one reality that counts, transcending all questions of success or failure within this world, thereby giving irrefragable evidence of its divine origin. The suffering forgiveness of love is ultimately victorious because it is no longer a merely human sacrifice: it has become one with the divine outpouring of self.

The mystery of grace that draws us toward participation in transcendent Being is one with the mystery of divine participation in human being. We recognize that the struggle between good and evil within every human heart and within history is part of the larger struggle. It is the divine grace that reaches into us that overcomes through its suffering love the power of evil. Our suffering endurance of the consequences of evil is one with the divine forgiveness beyond all limits. We know we are united with the definitive divine victory over evil and death. That is the deepest glimpse of the mystery vouchsafed to us. It does not dissolve the mystery of why or how or when the culmination will be reached, but it does provide a firm structure for the unfolding of our moral struggle. We are preserved from the imbalancing contemplation of an apocalyptic intervention or of nihilistic despair at the absurd abyss of failure. A steady focus on fulfilling our part to the utmost can be maintained in light of the assurance of the divine redemptive participation in our existence. Knowing the central meaning of the mystery in which we live, we can endure all of its uncertainties with peace.

The structure of this meditation may be Christian in resonance but it is not overtly so. Perhaps it could not be written except from the perspective of Christianity, but it can certainly be articulated without reference to the revelation of Christ. That is a strong indication of its wider representation. Its structure seems to be derived from and to be compatible with any of the transcendent world religions, because it does no more than follow out the direction in which they point, that is, that the outpouring of divine love is the means of overcoming the darkness of our hearts. Divine grace is the reality and evil knows itself as nothing in relation to it. The victory to be consummated at the end is already in place in the limitless gift of love. Only through the unmerited grace of love is the circle of destruction broken. Our submission to the way of redemptive suffering of evil is called forth by the divine redemptive suffering of evil. Moral reflections might point us in the direction of universal forgiveness but they would not have been confirmed without the recognition of the larger drama of divine forgiveness in which they are extended. This, however, raises a crucial question: If the redemptive significance of suffering can be extracted from our moral intimations and as reflected through the world religions, what is the significance of Christ? To put it another way, Is the historical Jesus necessary?

Christ Is Center

The first thing to be said is that the revelation of Christ renders the character of the redemptive drama unmistakably clear. Our own reflections and the elaborations of the world religions point in a similar direction, but it is hard to say that they reach it with the same definitive truth. The advance in differentiation which, we must always remember, is a differentiation of what has always been there, is not an insignificant event. It is not of merely secondary importance. The witness of Christ is not just a gain of intellectual clarity; it is the firm welding together of a structure that had only flimsily cohered up to that time and ever since. The most difficult and the deepest mystery of our existence now has definition. It is not eliminated nor even reduced, but its central structure is now confirmed. Confronted with the agonizing problem of evil and suffering in existence, of the contradiction between the imperative of virtue and the persistent failure of achievement, we can be assured that their resolution has already taken place. The fate is not only ours but the divine participation in our fate. That is what contains the certainty of redemption.

To have grasped that revelation with a clarity unsurpassed and accessible to even the lowliest individuals is no small addition. Yet we are nagged by the question, Have we lost the historical Jesus? Is this one more instance of withdrawing him behind the veil of philosophical speculation? Have we lost the divinity of his revelation? This is a serious objection since the tendency is a perennial one. It might even be valid if this was where our meditation were to end. But we cannot so lightly pass over the historical events or fail to recognize that they address us with a peculiar intensity of meaning. We recognize in the life, death, and resurrection of Jesus, as it has reached us in the historical record through the Church, confirmation of our deepest intuitions of order. In this sense we apprehend their truth by virtue of the same spiritual movement within ourselves. That is the mode by which we recognize the truth of any of the revelatory traditions: their symbols resonate with and extend our own experiences.

We not only confirm them, they confirm us. This is uniquely the case with Christ. His sacrifice of love not only bears witness to the divine participation in human suffering, but is itself the fullness of that participation manifested in a historical moment. More than a teacher and a symbol pointing toward a reality, Christ is the reality itself. This is the defense of the historical Jesus. It makes all the difference in the world to realize not only that the divine suffering of evil is the path of redemption, but that the fullness of that participation of God in the suffering of evil has historically taken place. In one sense it matters not at all to the principle of unlimited divine forgiveness. In another sense nothing is more crucial than to recognize that the fullness of its expression has occurred in a specific place and time. Redemption does not have to await its completion at the end of time. Now it can be recognized as definitively accomplished in that unique self-giving of God become man in Jesus. Participation in divine nature is not merely an aspiration, a continuation of the movement we experience within. Now it is a reality completed through the participation of transcendent divinity in human nature.

From this point on it becomes the means. The redemptive divine suffering of the consequences of evil has been fully revealed in the life and death of Jesus. From that fullness the transformative significance of the event radiates over the whole of history. It is truly the turning point because it is the moment in which the full transcendent mystery has been incarnated. As such, it is the center from which its influence extends throughout human existence from beginning to end. It is not a mere illustration or an event of more localized application; it is the full realization of the mystery that is therefore intended as the definitive transformation of creation itself. All that the world has awaited and still awaits has already been accomplished in those events. The transfiguration, by which we are drawn up to participate in the divine life, has already occurred, through the participation of transcendent divinity in our life. We do not await a more dramatic or more extensive divine intervention. The transfigurative process is complete. All we await is the patient unfolding of its mystery over time. For those who recognize the fullness of divine presence in Jesus, the central mystery is both revealed and consummated.

For those who do not share or do not know of that recognition, the same mystery, we have emphasized, is apprehended more darkly. The divine bending toward us in grace, the suffering participation in disorder, and the redemptive power of forgiveness are all themes that reverberate across the spiritual traditions of mankind. Indeed, when we ask what it is that enables men and women to recognize the truth of Christianity, it is ultimately explained by reference to what they already know within. They recognize the same divine presence, the same outpouring of love, in Christ as they sense through the expansive divine presence within themselves. It is not flesh and blood that reveals who Christ is, but the Father in heaven who draws us inwardly toward himself. If there were not a continuity between the pre-Christian traditions and Christianity, then there would be no way even to recognize what its revelation is all about. A wholly new revelation could hardly even be understood, let alone win a responsive acceptance.

Recognition Differs by Traditions

For that reason the revelation of Christ does not render the other spiritual traditions obsolete. Nor is it likely that their followers will abandon the heritage that has sustained them for millennia. There is an irreducible plurality among the traditions of the world that is not wholly transparent. Part of the mystery of our distribution as human beings in space and time must surely be the mystery of the plurality of spiritual outbursts and symbolic forms. But that does not mean that they do not share a common perspective. The more remarkable suggestion would be that one particular tradition or expression asserts a break from the broader movement. That would tend to signal an aberration since the claim to an exclusive possession of truth must always be treated with suspicion. Even though the human race exists under the influence of a moral fracture, even though it falls under the attraction of evil more frequently than it should, the power of the good has not by any means been removed as an ordering source in human experience. What is true or right may therefore be taken from the direction of people as a whole. The whole world judges rightly, Newman once noted, and the preference for being out of step is unlikely to be valid. The truth of Christianity is thus a truth confirmed in the world's spiritual traditions, not in any sense a departure from them. But this also means that their appeal continues and that the Christian advance cannot simply be expected to supplant them. The mystery of the plurality of sources of revelation continues even when the fullness of revelation has occurred.

The drama of recognition recurs and continues from one generation to the next as the interior movement of divine presence leads toward the recognition of its historically symbolized meaning. How the movement unfolds toward its self-recognition in symbols is very much dependent on the historically transmitted possibilities within the setting in which a person finds himself. This is why Muslims do not recount experiences of a Christian character or why Buddhists utilize their available symbols and are never likely to confuse themselves as discoverers of a Christian meaning. Each religious tradition has its characteristic experiences. They do not give expression to symbolic forms un-related to their background. But the relationship is not reducible to the simplistic model of cultural conditioning. What ultimately explains the appeal of the cultural forms purported to exercise such influence? Upon reflection, the relationship between individuals and the existing symbolic forms is more of a symbiotic one. Individuals are as crucial in supporting the inherited forms as the latter are in supporting them. The process is one in which the intimations of transcendent reality lead toward a revelatory opening whose character can scarcely be articulated. The struggle to find the appropriate symbols by which the experience itself can be retained in consciousness is a millennial struggle extending over the history of the race. No one generation has an absolute advantage in grasping the authoritative symbols, including even the generation that encountered Jesus in his physical presence. The search for the symbolic and conceptual evocation of the revelatory glimpses guiding us is a mysterious collaborative enterprise extending throughout human history. The plurality of centers of meaning is merely a reflection of our collaborative convergence toward truth.

What sustains both the separate traditions and the possibility of a conversation between them is the common sense of movement toward a reality beyond the human. It is the responsive movement toward transcendent reality that renders the symbols meaningful and is in turn sustained by the expressive unfolding of the symbols as well. The suggestion that all of this struggle to articulate the highest meaning available to human beings might be rooted in error or illusion does not agree with experience. Not only is it not possible to fool all of the people all of the time, but the objection fails on its own explanatory claims. Even if we were to grant that human beings can be deluded and are prone to project their longings into an ideal fulfillment beyond reach, how does that observation determine that this is indeed the case with the plurality of spiritual traditions universally present within history? And even more decisively, how can we explain the origin of such longings in the first place? What is it about the movement toward divine reality that is so attractive to such evidently material beings as ourselves? Projectionist psychologies explain everything except the need for explanation itself. There would not even be such a phenomenon if there were not first a sense of that higher reality whose attraction draws us in its pursuit.

What the projectionists are correct on is that the spiritual traditions cannot assure us of an answering response from the divine side. But that is in the nature of the revelatory encounter. We can have faith that God will reveal himself to all who open themselves toward him, and we can observe the regularity of its occurrence over time. Yet we cannot command the divine revelation. The new ingredient in the contemporary recognition of plural centers of revelation is the widespread presence of a nonrevelatory response. Our secular age implies the existence of large social strata to whom God is no longer present. He does not reveal himself to them or they are not capable of hearing his voice. That is the real source of the projectionist critique. We live in an age in which for many people the question of God has become irrelevant. There are many sources for the phenomenon but its crucial significance is the crisis of meaning it has spawned. Without a transcendent measure all other measures stand exposed as relative and contrived. We are left without any point of reference. For a great many people in our day the horizon of mystery guarding our existence appears as an increasingly ominous cloud barely concealing the blackness and blankness beyond. The test of any meditation that attempts to open the path of meaning in the present is that it does not shy away from the challenge of the death of God. How is it possible to discover, not simply construct, meaning in a world from which God is experienced as effectively absent?

CHAPTER 5

THE END OF THE MODERN WORLD

T HE MODERN secular world seems to exclude a transcendent source of meaning in principle. This appears to be what constitutes its self-understanding, that secular civilization is capable of providing its own meaning without reference to an order of being beyond itself. Of course, religious perspectives can continue as private enclaves of meaning, but they cannot expect to receive any substantive public recognition. To do so would be to jeopardize the whole modern conception of a self-contained world separated out from its previous theological presuppositions. The secular world demands the privatization of religion, and that in turn removes the authoritative public recognition of transcendent truth. Only what can be expressed in the bounded language of secular ends and means can acquire public status. The triumph of the secular spirit in building a civilization preoccupied with the successes and satisfactions of this life is evident in the global rush for economic development. Secularism seems to have won.

The only difficulty is that the victory is marred by the inability of the secular spirit to eliminate all dissatisfaction. The impressive sweep of the secular ethos that calls us to build a human order of development and fulfillment within this life is undeniable. But equally persistent have been the voices of discontent with this project. It has not finally been possible for the blandishments of a secular paradise to still the longings for a higher divine paradise. Rather than subduing the movement of faith, or at least taming and restricting it to a private sphere, our late modern world has seen the resurgence of religious movements on a global scale. An increasing assertiveness by various religionists is the single most salient fact of political life both at home and abroad. Whether it is the rise of the Christian Right in the United States or Islamic militantism in the Middle East and elsewhere, or the less raucous manifestations of a renewed spirit of religious fervor and a pervasive interest in spirituality, the direction is clearly away from all that the modern world has promised. They represent decisive rejections of the secular project and impressive reaffirmations of the transcendent dynamic of human existence. But they are also deeply confused about their continuing relationship to the modern world. Having found their own truth, the rediscoverers of the spirit now must work out how it relates to the social and historical setting in which they find themselves.

Even the discovery of God does not lift us out of this world. For as long as he wills it we must remain in this life to work out as best we can the meaning and direction we must follow within it. The light of transcendent illumination is a piercing beam from beyond, but it does not illuminate the surrounding area. The mystery of the whole remains. The difficulty of articulating the consequences of revelation for the modern secular world is evident in the confusion concerning the relationship between religion and politics. Does the personal experience of being "born again" suggest that we must work to bring about a "reborn" political order? If Jesus is my Lord and Savior, should I work to make America once again an exclusively Christian nation? What is the role of Christians in a constitutional order that is framed by the prohibition against established religion? If Allah is the one truth, then why must we tolerate those who deny his authority? How is it possible to separate the law of Islam from the man-made law of the state? These are all good questions, and the fact that they have not resulted in good answers indicates the difficulty entailed. It is not enough to have been touched by divine grace; to make sense of our situation we must have some understanding of the context within which we find ourselves. Only then will we find the common language to speak with one another and only then can the transcendent source of meaning have any chance of acquiring public recognition.

Spiritual Heart of the Secular

The problem with the religious and spiritual revivalists is that they have approached communication from the perspective of their own experience. They are bringing a great illumination to a dark and hostile secular world. Inevitably they conceive the process as confrontation. But in reality they have nothing to fear from that monolithic secular power, for it has never been what it appeared to be. The truth is that the closed secular world has never even existed. At best it was a project that was inconclusive, but it could not be concluded because it was impossible. Rather than suspiciously searching for ways to inject spiritual influence into the secular world, the revivalists might find a more effective strategy in a sympathetic reading of that world itself. Then the two sides might discover they have more in common than they thought. The search for a common language and for a balance between them is not as insuperable as it appeared. Tension is dramatically reduced through the realization that it is not so much a matter of finding a place for transcendent illumination within the secular frame of reference, as it is of understanding why the secular world has never really existed except in aspiration. The two sides might then meet in the recognition that they point in the same direction.

The closed secular world has never existed because, as we have seen, no meaning is possible on those terms. All that constitutes the vitality of human life, the whole source of interest, is derived from what draws us on beyond the present limits. All that is finished and complete is drained of significance for us. We find it intolerable to live within the homogenous limits of what is destined to remain forever the same. To the extent that a secular frame of reference means such contraction, it cannot support human life. What has made a secular world possible has been its capacity to draw us onward through the mysterious promise of a future that transcends our past. Its whole secret has been its ability to persuade us that we are moving toward a state that will be qualitatively better and different than that in which we are now. That is, a secular ethos trades on the residue of transcendent longing and mystery still present within us even if we no longer accept the spiritual articulation of that movement. As soon as we recognize that there is no great or glorious future awaiting us, that the satisfactions we possess now are the best that can be attained in the future, that we are literally going nowhere, the whole project is undermined. The secular emperor is revealed to have no clothes. That collapse of the modern project is the source of the disorientation we now encounter in our civilization. But it need not unfold into a mood of terminal glumness if we can discover what it was that first drew us onto a path doomed for failure.

What was it that drew us in search of a will-o'-the-wisp? If we can understand the source of attraction that drove us, then we can have a better prospect of reorienting ourselves toward its real source. We must break the hold of our addictions by understanding the nature of our susceptibility. For the modern world that driving impulse can be summarized in one abiding inclination: the search for transcendent fulfillment within this life. All that has been the source of human longing, the search for infinite perfection and fulfillment, is expected to be found within this world. The mysterious pull of transcendent Being is transferred to immanent reality. Eternity is replaced by the future as the region toward which our whole existence is directed. The movement toward higher reality, a fuller transcendent life, is now directed toward the point within time when we will have overleaped the ordinary into the newly transfigured state of being. In other words, the modern world is still characterized as a journey toward a goal not yet attained. But that goal is conceived as a goal definitively contained within this world.

How this shift toward an immanent eschaton came about is a rather complicated story whose details are still in dispute among scholars. What all do agree on is that the modern world is defined by its intramundane focus and that it understands itself as a departure from the preceding medieval emphasis on transcendent fulfillment. It is this shift that accounts for the extraordinary release of energy that has characterized the modern world. Even a term like "development," which has come to characterize the difference between rich and poor countries, is related to this source. It is not that all poor countries lack natural resources or even access to technology or even capital for investment. The single most important factor contributing to a country's "development" is the attitude of its people. Are they driven by that feverish concentration of energy that makes success in this life the one absolute necessity? Or are they content to live within the natural rhythms of life and death as their traditions have taught for generations? We are all aware of the difference between the spiritual maturity and depth of many traditional societies, which contrasts strongly with the frenzied and disoriented pace of life in the more developed world. Yet it is in the latter that advances in the standard of living occur. Modernity presents us with the paradox of a civilization that advances and declines at the same time.

Paradox of Advance and Decline

The spectacular achievements of rational technological civilization are undeniable. Success in controlling the forces of nature and directing them toward the service of human life is no small achievement. The progressive improvement of the conditions of life for billions of human beings, a process that is still continuing exponentially, is surely of historic significance. Whether it is the dramatic expansion of agriculture, the burgeoning technologies of communication and calculation, the epochal achievements in controlling and eliminating disease, or the generation of wealth and leisure for the large mass of societies, the benefits to humanity are vast and palpable. No one could wish to return to a less advanced era—or at least no one who took a moment to reflect on the cost of such a return in terms of the human suffering and death it would entail. Yet there persists a nagging question about the cost of development itself: What is the condition on which it has all been made possible?

It is surely the belief in progress itself. We must believe that progress is possible and that it is the supreme value of human life. Without that unhesitating certainty we would not have expended our efforts in such a single-minded direction and the results would not have been as impressive. If human beings are to give their all in building this better world, then they must be moved by the conviction that it deserves their undivided effort. The incremental advances in controlling nature through science, technology, and industry do not occur easily. Nature will yield control only to those indomitable enough to wrest the secrets from her. It is not a task for the fainthearted or distracted. If there is the slightest uncertainty that this is the one direction guaranteed to lead toward our goal, then we will not have the energy to sustain the almost superhuman effort that must often be expended in the great production and engineering feats of the modern world. The transfer of transcendent fulfillment toward an intramundane achievement must be complete.

The cost of the dedication required to build the modern world is, in other words, spiritual disorientation. This is the dimension of decline inherent in the process. It is spiritual disorientation because the goal does not exist. The more we approach it, the more it recedes from our grasp, since no attainment is capable of filling the longing for infinite perfection that draws us. Even worse, its attainment, if it were possible, would not mean mankind's arrival at unlimited happiness. It would be an unmitigated disaster. Utopia is the dead end of human life, as is all perfection, because it means the end of the moving search that is the whole vitality of our lives. Without dissatisfaction, without inquiry, without unlimited reaching out, there would be nothing left for which to live. Our lives would literally be over. All consciousness, reflection, poetry, conversation, and love would cease. The only thing left would be the dumb silence of animal contentment. Transcendent fulfillment cannot be transferred to this world because nothing in this life is capable of supplying unlimited life and because without the transcendent dynamic of our existence we would no longer be human beings.

The vacuity of the goal of the modern world is its great secret. All of its success depends on our capacity to ignore the nonexistence of that at which we aim. But it is an unstable arrangement. Eventually the two sides must collide. The enormous energy expended in moving toward it must encounter the realization that it does not and cannot exist. We cannot simultaneously keep a goal constantly before us and fail to become aware of what that goal is. Sooner or later the shock of self-awareness must occur. We realize that we have been chasing a chimera, that we have been cheated, and that all our expense of effort has been for nothing. That is a particularly vulnerable moment because the loss of faith leaves us with nothing. We cannot simply shift our allegiance toward some other intramundane goal. Once we realize that nothing in the secular world is capable of providing our transcendent fulfillment, we are utterly deprived of sustaining purpose or control. We realize that the vaunted power at our disposal in the modern world is truly the most powerless. We have no object to guide its use.

This is the self-realization that characterizes our present historical moment. It has much to do with the fading of the bloom on the idea of progress. Strikingly absent are the heady expectations of the future as an expanse of unlimited improvement, moving toward ever higher levels of human happiness and perfection. Now we are much more likely to reflect on the unintended consequences of progress and to suspect that it will bring as many problems as it solves. Gone is the excitement that greeted each previous development of technology as harbingers of an unlimited future. In its place is a weariness and wariness that seems to know that all we will have obtained is a new level of gadgetry. High-definition TV and the World Wide Web cannot in the end provide the human fulfillment for which we long; indeed, they may even get in the way by adding a new layer of complexity and expense. All that technological development can provide is access to newer and better tools. They are no longer greeted as confirmation of the final spiritual fulfillment that awaits us. It is this evaporation of the faith in progress that is the most crucial dimension of our time.

Nowhere was this turn more dramatic than in the collapse of the most militant forms of the progressivist faith. The great ideological movements that had elaborated the most strident form of the myth finally spent their impulse at the end of the twentieth century. Movements like nationalism, racism, national socialism, fascism, anarchism, and communism had been the dynamic forces on the world scene for a long time. They seemed to possess a particularly virulent strain of the modern impulse toward historical transfiguration. Their more moderate competitors and opponents, especially of the liberal democratic variety, seemed incapable of evoking the same intensity of commitment. Faced by the white heat of revolutions and purges, nothing seemed to match their "hideous strength." But then one by one they fell apart under the force of their own frenzy and destroyed themselves against the rocks of reality. The last and most successful of these movements, communism, came crashing down literally and symbolically with the fall of the Berlin Wall in 1989. With the disappearance of its power communism lost its legitimation as the wave of the future. It stood exposed as the hollow wreck it had always been. Only now it was relegated to the past.

No wonder such events have sharpened our sense of living at a turning point in the modern world. Now it is commonplace to refer to our era as "postmodern." The entire modern project, the movement toward an intramundane goal to be reached through indomitable human effort, has been discredited. The goal has been exposed as an illusion. The effort to reach it through revolutionary violence has accomplished nothing but a holocaust of misery. Even the more gradual route of economic and technological progress has been seen to carry its own not insignificant costs. A shattering of the modern self-confidence has been the result. It is one thing to celebrate the disappearance of oppressive regimes and the restraining of technological excesses, but to realize that we have nothing more compelling to put in their place imposes a sobering tone on the whole realization. We have lost not just an important political movement but the legitimating myth of our world. If there is no bright shining future that beckons us, then what can provide meaning to our lives?

This is the "crisis of meaning" so much discussed by philosophers ever since Nietzsche employed the term "nihilism" to describe it. All that has changed since his time is that the self-awareness has become public. That is the context of this book and the reason why it had to take the form of a meditation from the most elementary reflections available. All discourse at present exists under the shadow of the abyss of nihilism that hangs over all meaning for us. Deconstruction is merely a contemporary technique of exposing the groundlessness of all assertions. It merely brings the problem to our awareness. But the real source of nihilism is that the sustaining myth of the modern world has disappeared. Without the assurance of a larger horizon of meaning that signifies and sustains our efforts, everything falls apart. Nothing means anything and nothing is worth doing. The horizon of mystery that seemed to draw us has turned out to be a mirage and we no longer have the confidence to discern any other defining boundary to our existence.

False Absolutes from True

Yet even the false absolutes of technological control or world communism would never have had an effect on us if we were not drawn toward a horizon of transcendence. Even to be mistaken in the object of our longings we must already be drawn by that of which we are in search. It is not enough to say that such aspirations are merely the residue of a religious past and that we are now better off to swear a plague on both their houses, religious and secular. No, the longing for total revolution we have witnessed is no mere echo of a vanished world. It had a drive and intensity precisely because it spoke to the deepest sense of who we are. The force of this aspiration toward another level of reality, which has been the source of the entire modern creative and destructive movements, testifies to the persistence of the transcendent attraction. Even when the traditional religious formulations have become opaque men would prefer to pin their hopes on an illusory transcendence than live within the prison of the everyday. That is the deepest level of the pathos that has gripped the modern world.

It is not a discovery of recent years that communism did not work or that technology failed to deliver on its promises. Everyone knew (or sensed) this truth from the start. What needs to be explained is less the collapse of communism than its survival for so long in the face of such evident failure. Nor is it a unique discovery that material and technical progress does not provide any advance in human fulfillment. Every consumer can report such an experience once the excitement of the day of purchase has worn off. We buy a new camera, a new refrigerator, a new car, or even a new house, but we are no happier in any qualitative sense than before. What needs to be explained is how we have preserved the faith that this steady accumulation of possessions would lead to some morally radiant future. What was it that suckered us as a whole civilization into a joyless pursuit of joy? Surely it was that the dream of progress, in its revolutionary or evolutionary guises, traded on the real thing. But in order for a masquerade to be successful we must already have at least an elementary sense of the reality it portrays. This is why dogs never lose themselves in false ideologies. It is first necessary to live in continuity with a reality that is not present and that is known only in that mode.

Transformational ideologies would have had no appeal if they did not speak to a profound disposition within human beings. One cannot move whole societies and provide the underlying dynamic for a civilization without touching the deepest level of the human soul. The superficial wish that we did not have such transcendent intimations or that we might be able to ignore them cannot change the fundamental condition. Indeed, the call for restraint itself is already the beginning of an effort to live within an order of limits that presupposes an awareness of the unlimited that is denied to us. At its best such calls to live the only finite existence available to us depend on preserving the sense of distance from transcendent life. The source of its appeal is that restraint is the way toward order and dignity. We may not have access to transfiguration but we can stand firmly on the side of honesty and respect for limits. But that too is an appeal to a value that is unlimited. It compels or draws us irrespective of the tangible limited benefits it provides. Sure, the reason for restraint is so that we no longer wear ourselves out in an orgy of self-destruction, as we would under the influence of an addiction. But its attraction is that we gain thereby not merely a life of peace and order, but the incomparable value of having lived in accordance with what is right. We have thus regained the road to true transcendence.

That is ultimately the promise that remains of the debacle of modern civilization, which seems to have exhausted itself in the pursuit of futility. The gloom of postmodernity that hangs over it at present might then be lifted as we perceive the bright sunshine on the other side. Our regret must not be that we pursued the impossible ideal of transfiguration. Rather, it is that we sought it in a way we should not have sought it and we knew the deception attempted thereby. That is the repentance that is in order for the limitless cruelty, the evil of this most evil century. The holocausts of our time cannot be dismissed as accidental events, regrettable but incidental to the larger ideals of our civilization. On the contrary, they are intimately connected. The confidence that we were serving the great humanitarian goal of history provided a license for the perpetration of anything we felt or were told was justified. All that mattered was that we were self-perceived idealists acting only out of the most exalted motives. The great ideological movements provided the moral cover for unlimited evil. Holocausts are the inevitable outcome of the conceit that men are now in charge of the resolution of the problems of existence. Spiritual transformation that can only be sought through submission to inexorable divine goodness was to be realized more effectively through the violence of revolutionary action.

It was not the ideals that were at fault but the self-deception that they could be short-circuited. By impatience at the only means available for spiritual growth, the arduous struggle to realize the intimations of goodness disclosed within us, we corrupted the very ideals themselves. We demonstrated that we were not serious about fidelity to moral truth. It was more important for us to reach the self-satisfaction of our own righteousness than to actually be righteous. We traded the incidental good feeling of morality for the reality itself. Eventually it mattered not at all what means we employed so long as they guaranteed that we would reach that superior vantage point from which we could look down on all previous existence. Unwilling to be men, we sought to become God, only without submitting to the only way he has ordained for us to participate in his nature. To ensure the finality of our victory it became necessary to eliminate God too. In the secular messianic movements of the past two hundred years the madness of free creaturely existence reached its apogee.

It would not be correct to say that we have now finally recovered from it. In truth, we have merely exhausted the obsession. For the moment it is past, but we have not as yet found our way back to the order from which we slipped because we have not yet comprehended the roots of the disorder itself. It is not enough to regard the cataclysmic horrors through which we have passed as some great disaster from which we are now gratefully separated. This is one of the abiding tendencies in all of the efforts to "remember" the holocausts of the century. They cannot be properly "remembered" until we can understand how they have been possible, that is, to comprehend how it was possible for ordinary men and women to participate willingly in their perpetration. The mystery of the holocausts can only be probed when we have understood the same potential abyss within our own hearts. We must be able to recognize ourselves in both the victims and the executioners: There but for the grace of God go I. Then we will have some measure of the extraordinary spiritual forces that swirl around us and then we will appreciate the extent to which we must play our part in the larger struggle between good and evil beyond us. We are not free to reorder the drama at will.

Even the impatient impulse to reach the heights of divinity by violence is a response to the pull of transcendent being, albeit a perverse reflection of it. There would be no restless thrusting out beyond limits if there were not already the awareness of the unlimited as the goal deep within us. The appeal of the ideological movements, with their apocalyptic visions of sacrifice and destruction, had nothing to do with tangible material rewards or improvements. At their core they promised their followers salvation, contact with the redeeming and transforming higher reality. Their quasi-religious character has long been recognized, despite their avowedly atheistic stance. Indeed, Marx would not have made the rejection of God so central to his system if he had not sensed the extent to which the self-divinization of man required it. Man can reach the heights of divinity only if there is no God already preempting that primacy of place. The only difficulty is that with the disappearance of God man now has no means of moving toward a fullness of being presently beyond his reach. How can he pull himself up by his own bootstraps? The self-transparent futility of the exercise reveals an abyss of darkness that stretches the bounds of credibility. Why would Marx or Nietzsche or Freud or Comte persist in a project whose futility was apparent?

Transfiguration Only from God

No satisfactory answer can ultimately be given to such a question, one that is at the core of all self-destructive obsessions. The addiction must ultimately be broken by the touch of a reawakening reality. The blindness, the obstinacy in the face of impossibility, the will to persist even if they are wrong, to use the formulation of Ivan Karamazov, can only be dissolved by the grace that melts the hardness of hearts. Nor is that miraculous touch so far away. This is the poignancy of the modern revolt against God: it is a revolt inspired by the longing for divine life. All that is required is an awakening to the presence of that reality that draws us into the quest even in a distorted form. The thirst for transformation, for a fulfillment within history, for an ecstatic leap into transcendence would never have occurred unless we were already aware of the goal within. The mistake was to imagine that we could achieve it by force and on our own terms. The remedy is the realization that the reality that draws us is beyond us, is transcendent. It can only be reached through the acceptance of the gift of divine being that reaches into our lives. The only route to the divinization of man is through the grace of God who makes us sharers in his divine nature. Only God can make us divine.

At that point the revolt is dissolved. The whole titanic striving that drove the modern world to become its own complete creator falls away. We realize that what drew us toward the revolutionary ideal was the echo it contained of the inner spiritual revolution we sought. For many human beings it was the closest they came to the higher aspiration, since the traditional carriers of spiritual meaning, religious communities, had become opaque as symbols of the truth. It was a hard lesson to discover the abyss of cruelty that infiltrated an idealism unconnected to the submission to divine truth. So long as it was based on the conceit of human self-supremacy, nothing stood in the way of the will to dominate over others. When there is no divine judge to measure our actions, then all restraints we choose to impose are merely arbitrary: everything is permitted. The most exalted ideals, aimed at the most passionate evocations of justice and brotherhood, cannot withstand the endless rationalizations of cruelty. When we are the ones who decide what is right, then no one can be permitted to stand in our way. The conclusion is that the nightmare of inhumanity betrays the humanitarian inspiration from which it began.

But it does not have to end in the despair of all ideals. The false manipulation of truth would not have been possible unless there had been a truth at the beginning. Even more, we would not now be able to recognize the mendacity of the ideological swindle, promising justice through the commission of massive injustice, unless we still possessed a strong sense of the transcendent boundary that cannot be breached. Besides discrediting all idealistic evocations, an equally pervasive outcome has been the heightening of the sense of limits that have been massively exceeded. The outrages to humanity provoke an awakening of the order that guards and sustains our human nature. Man's railing against all limits recalls to consciousness the constancy of such limits. Resistance to evil deepens our participation in goodness. The process of opposing the falsity of all appeals at hollow absolutes delineates the awareness of the concrete character of the responsibilities we owe one another. We recognize that we play our part within a transcendent drama of which we are not the source. The attempt to assume control of the whole works not toward the benefit of humanity but only to the destruction of the concrete human beings whose lives we affect.

We recognize that the only justice or order that is possible for us depends on the recognition of the mysterious limits of the context in which it occurs. The urge to impose a total solution, taking comprehensive responsibility for the perfection of all things, accomplishes nothing but the abyss. If we wish to avoid the catastrophe, then we must be content to do what we can under the realization that we are not the authors of the drama nor responsible for its final resolution. The only way not to botch our roles is to follow the intimations that are given to us. We cannot get behind the given toward any more fundamental level because it is submission to the obligations that disclose themselves in our lives that is the route to that higher level of being. The mysterious sustaining reality of the drama, which we stand to lose or gain through our enactments, is the reliable source of our assurance. We can trust in the role we have been given because we have come to recognize it as the reality that preserves us from the abyss. The sustaining presence is revealed as the mysterious fullness toward which we are drawn. No matter how distorted the ideals may have become, the movement of resistance to their deforming influence arises from the still point of transcendence that survives.

What enables us to judge the gap between ideal and reality is that we continue to possess the reality of the ideal. There is no getting behind the elementary sense of what is right in order to arrive at something prior. In that inexorable limit of mystery in which we participate lies the whole secret of our preservation. It has not been left up to us to determine the line between good and evil. Before we ever reflect on it the awareness of a limit is present and unfolds as the starting point of all our reflections. However much we may have lost our connection to that imperishable order, we are never utterly cut off from its saving guidance. We know when we have done wrong. That troubling undertow of which we would often prefer to be rid is the thin line of contact with the higher life we constantly seek. By responding to its pressure we discern the direction we should follow and we discover our growing participation in transcendent reality. We are lifted into the truly immortal and saved from the illusory immortality of our dreams.

This is a development that has increasingly occurred through the struggle with the abyss of the modern world. Those who have resisted the might of the totalitarian state, with its emancipatory ideology and its inhumanitarian reality, bear witness to the true inner transformation. They discovered within themselves a power greater than the illusory strength of ideology. They possessed the reality of transcendent being and could overcome the deprivations inflicted upon them by its shadow political expression. One of the remarkable aspects of the twentieth century is the process of spiritual deepening and awakening that occurred in societies that seemed to have reduced human beings to absolute zero. The "power of the powerless" is a title of one of Václav Havel's essays but it might well stand for the witness of all the heroes of the totalitarian struggle. A depth beyond all telling enabled them to emerge victorious even in death.

It is one of the supreme ironies of the century we are leaving behind that its most total effort to impose a secular order on existence has provoked the most extensive revival of spirituality. Most observers note the coincidence but fail to comprehend their interrelationship. In fact they are correlative, for it is precisely the effort to eliminate the transcendent drive of the human spirit so definitively that uncovers its immovable presence in human life. We are alerted to what is at stake: the loss of that transcendent mystery constituting the whole dynamic of our existence. A hollow rhetorical shell is no substitute. Even gaining the whole utopian fulfillment espoused by the ideologies cannot justify the loss of all our moral worth. If we have become moral zeros, then no historical achievements mean anything. Ultimately the value of everything for us is measured by a reality that transcends history itself.

Good and Evil Outweigh History

We do not live *within* history anymore than we live *within* a secular world. The context of our lives is ultimately defined by an openness to transcendent reality, and it is there that the question of meaning is decided. Have we lived in accordance with what is right beyond all calculation of interest or contribution? It matters little whether the schemes we have proposed accomplish much or little. The real question is, Have they been pursued rightly or wrongly? Have we been faithful to the larger order of goodness or have we betrayed its truth for the sake of our preoccupation with short-term gains? The disappearance of the megalomaniacal schemes of universal historical perfection and the fading of the bloom from the more moderate incremental perfectionism of technology remind us of the context of significance in which we really do live. It is not defined by intramundane achievements, however important they may be. On the contrary, worldly accomplishments derive their significance from their subordination to an order of eternal value. If we lose sight of that transcendent goal, then we lose all that makes life worth living. Our accomplishments turn to dust.

The realization that the closed secular world is a wasteland is not the death of meaning. It is its beginning. We become aware of the vacuum only in light of the transcendent fullness of meaning. To regain contact with the illuminative beyond, all that is required is that we reflect on the source of our dissatisfaction. What is it that heightens the awareness of emptiness? Is there not at the back of it some sense of the fullness, a fullness without limit, that should be present? How indeed can we know about that higher perfection if we do not already possess some sense of it? Why is it that we cannot rest within a world of limits, one whose meaning eventually comes to an end? The very questions contain that which we seek. We cannot get back beyond the awareness of our tension toward transcendent reality. It is as much a part of the given as the realization of the imperfection and finitude of all that we encounter. Meaning is a problem for us only because we sense a fullness of reality toward which we are drawn. The crucial question is, Can it be more than an irresolvable source of frustration? Granted that the secular world is driven by the quest for a meaning it cannot provide, is there any way in which the meaning it seeks can be provided?

The answer would be no if human existence were a static reality. But our consciousness is not a fixed quantity. It is capable of amplification or contraction depending on our response. Contact with transcendent mystery can be regained if we follow the invitation revealed within our restlessness. By pursuing the presence that appears only as the irritating boundary of our consciousness, the sting that will not let us rest content with all our hard-won achievements and possessions, we open ourselves to the fuller reception of its reality. In that moment beyond our control the miracle of revelation can occur. We sense ourselves being drawn into a fuller and deeper encounter with the mystery that had been at the boundary of our existence all along. Now the process becomes self-sustaining. Much less effort is required of us as we are pulled into a more real reality than anything we had known before. We know that this is the truth. There is a measure of meaning and value as certain, as invincible, as eternal as our longing. In that glimpse we are graced by the touch of transcendent Being. With veiled eyes we brush against God. Then it is over and we struggle to take away from it what we have learned.

A growth of the soul has occurred by which we were stretched beyond the finite limits of all existence. In that brief extension of ourselves we were made sharers in the divine life. We knew it. Then we returned to this measured and limited world, where everything has an end. Nothing has changed except us. Even we are not that much different beyond possessing the memory of that other reality that is the guarantee of meaning. The dissatisfaction and meaningless limitation of everything we know is not the final reality. They are contained within the fullness of being we have encountered. We have no more than that assurance. The frustration with earthly existence is made clearer, and now we understand the irritating tug at the boundary of our consciousness. But now too the tension becomes supportable through the memory of that other reality beyond. Neither we nor the world are different. Only a clearer illumination of the measure, the source of meaning in transcendent reality, has been revealed. That is all.

Transparence of Existence

What makes it sufficient is the realization that we are not cut off from the goal we seek. It is there, it has revealed itself, and it will reveal itself again to us. By responding to its invitation through faith we know that the dynamic of our existence will be enlarged to glimpse again its ineffable joy. All we have to do is respond. Then we are drawn into a process that opens us up beyond a level we had ever thought possible at the beginning. The everyday self falls away and for a brief time we are lifted into the life of that higher being that is all illumination. What had been opaque and burdensome at the beginning of the struggle suddenly becomes transparent and easy. We are drawn into the fullness of divine mystery which bends itself toward us so long as our trusting response continues. The process cannot be under our control, since we cannot lift ourselves up beyond ourselves, but it is crucially dependent on our willingness to follow the intimations by which we are drawn. Only through our willingness to submit to the divine will does the divine will disclose itself to us. We must be willing to be opened for the opening to occur.

The process is paralleled by the dynamic enlargement of our spirits when we play a piece of music or act in a drama. At the beginning we may feel somewhat cold and diffident about the task. The prospect may even bore us. But as we take the first steps the stirring of vitality begins to occur. Gradually we are drawn bit by bit into a deeper involvement. We feel ourselves being stretched and we reach further than we had first felt capable. Soon the power of the music or the drama takes over and we are no longer doing the main work. It is being done to us. We are lifted beyond ourselves and are moving easily over all of its notes or lines. We find ourselves capable of a kind of playing or acting we had never suspected was within us. We surprise ourselves and wonder afterward if we could ever play the piece or act the part again as well, just as we were doubtful at the beginning if we could reach the heights that on other occasions had been attained. But here it is again. Having gone through the whole buildup we are back again at the maximum extension of our abilities. The white-heat intensity takes over and for a moment our feet leave the earth. We are in another realm. Then we return, back on the solid ground, the piece or the play is over and our life goes on—until the next time.

In other words, that dynamic of experience is not so unusual. It is, after all, why people watch or participate in sports or lose themselves in the excitement of movies and books. The quasi-religious character of such peak experiences, which occur most substantively in the intimate relationships of human life, provide the whole texture of meaning. Falling in love is so powerful and ubiquitous a preoccupation of human beings precisely because it is one of the defining jumps into a higher order of being. This is why many long for it so much they end up seeking to renew it endlessly through successive affairs. But they discover that the experience is not ours to possess and subordinate to our personal gratification. It can only be had on its own terms, which includes the recognition of its singular call on us. The more loves we pursue, the less they can each be loved. Perhaps this is why the birth of children is the other great transformative experience of human life, for they give a solidity and permanence that is inescapable to the love between the parents. Each of us experiences such events as if we were the first human beings to have encountered their profound impact. Nothing prepares us for the surprise. Relationships of encompassing love are such out-of-the-ordinary experiences that they cannot easily be communicated to those who have not had them. Certainly none of their inner transformative power can be conveyed except metaphorically. It is only because others can and do have them that they can be communicated.

That possibility is rooted in the open dynamic of human existence. It is capable of wide expansion or contraction. Fundamentally, we might say that it is the transcendent tension at the core of human life that is the source of the amplitude. It is because human beings are directed toward a reality beyond all limits that experiences in which they are lifted into a higher realm are so important to them. The sacredness of falling in love and loving a child arises from the spiritual propensity already present. It is not simply that such dramatic enlargements of our heart are metaphors for the final enlargement of our soul. They are only possible because we are incomplete beings in search of the fulfillment that will complete us. One of the great dangers of a secular worldview is that we will mistake the peak experiences that occur in our lives for the final goal of our existence. Human relationships will then be invested with a burden too heavy for them to bear and they will suffer inevitable deformation from the weight imposed on them. Neither our spouses nor our children nor our friends can stand for transcendent perfection, however admirable they may be. It is all the more important therefore to see that the expansive relationships and moments of our life point toward and have their fulfillment only within the movement toward the ultimately transfigurative goal. They are made possible by the transcendent openness of who we are.

In this way even the high points of secular life are preserved from distortion by understanding the gap between aspiration and fulfillment. Without a boundary context the secular world is in perpetual danger of exaggerating and wearing itself out in an impossible quest. How can the unattainability of our goal be accepted if we do not recognize its transcendent character? By searching for the infinite within the finite we set ourselves up for endless disappointment. This is the despair of meaning in which we presently find ourselves as a civilization. The irony is that the answer is not far away. We have only to recognize the radically transcendent direction of our longing to realize that no immanent attainments are capable of fulfilling it. Secular self-understanding is on the verge of that recognition. At least we are no longer seriously pursuing historical progress as an absolute. We know the unsatisfactory limitations of all we are going to encounter. All that it takes is the courage or the faith to enter on the first halting steps of openness toward the transcendent drama that pulls so forcefully upon us. Then we will be on our way toward the illuminative leap we can rely upon occurring because it has already happened before.

The mood of depression evoked by the end of the modern world, the failure of the secular experiment in meaning, we now recognize as misplaced. We are instead relieved that perfection has not been reached within history or that human beings have not been able to construct the definitive meaning of existence. The oppressiveness of the failure now turns out to be our liberation. Through the collapse of the secular experiment our humanity is saved. Now our horizon is bounded by the mystery of transcendent fulfillment, not by the historical march toward a point of closed contentment within time. Instead we remain open, free, and guided by the intimations of a reality equidistant from all human beings because it is eternal. The secular world is no more because we look on it as secular, that is, from a perspective radically outside of it. This is the secret of the present historical moment. All the fretting about the end of modernity, the collapse of secular projects and meaning, is made possible by the realization that we have passed beyond it. We are back at the original meaning of *secular*, that is, what can be separated from the spiritual. The deepest truth of our age is not that the modern world is over but that we have already passed into the transcendent perspective that enables us to view it as limited. The death of the modern project has reawakened us to eternity.

The meditative answer to the riddle of modern nihilism is of course not the same as the advent of a transcendent reorientation of our civilization. Individual insights must find a way of becoming publicly authoritative for that transformation to occur. That is the reflection of the following two chapters on politics and on culture. The mystery of nonfulfillment that seemed to frustrate the modern impetus toward a secular terrestrial paradise has now been discovered as the mystery that guarded our humanity from the most horrific distortions. The totalitarian states were the ultimate expression of that failed experiment. Now we have begun to appreciate the finiteness of our capacities and the intractable character of the reality within which we find ourselves. We cannot change the world as Marx proposed. To those who have not been overcome by disappointment this appears as the beginning of our liberation. We are on the way toward a rediscovery of a richness, of an expansiveness of meaning largely absent from the preceding century. Our openness is constituted by the touch of truly transcendent Being, not false absolutes. The question that remains is, Can that openness be embraced in a new civilizational affirmation?

CHAPTER 6

THE POLITICS OF LIBERTY

W E H A V E seen that meaning can only be anchored in the relationship to transcendent mystery. All other boundaries dissolve before the relentless dynamic of human questions and aspirations. Finite frames of reference positively invite the movement beyond them. Nothing endures if it is rooted only in the finite secular world. This realization is tantamount to signifying the end of the modern world which has been posited on the possibility of an entirely constructed world of meaning. The only success it has had has traded on the residual sense of transcendent mystery that still attached to the great heroic enterprises of human effort. Once it became apparent that neither technology nor revolution delivered on their promise of transfiguration, their inspirational appeal fell away. We are left in the dead end of a secular world without meaning that is now irrevocably closed to the only source of meaning that can sustain it. How is it possible for transcendent Being to penetrate the secular boredom of the world?

Part of the answer, we have seen, is that such secular boredom is not a mood of unvarying permanence. It is shot through with the awareness of its own restless movement toward the transcendence that has even inspired the development of intramundane counterfeits. But there is also the possibility of rediscovering the germ of transcendent openness secreted within the only success-ful order to emerge within that world. Modernity has not been a history of unmitigated failure. Success has not been confined to the narrow band of technological progress. A viable social and political order of impressive moral stature and striking historical durability has also emerged. The unselfconsciousness of this order and its characteristic modesty have stood in the way of the full recognition of its genius. But it is nevertheless the one tan-gible success story in modern political theory and practice. It hardly has a definite name but has at various times been called the "constitutional," the "Whig," the "republican," the "liberal," or the "democratic" tradition. By whatever designation, we recog-nize its central illumination of the inviolable liberty and dignity of the individual.

That is the spark of transcendent meaning firmly embedded within our secular world. In contrast to the false absolutes of ideology, the transcendent worth of each individual is a rock of enduring solidity. The collectivist willingness to sacrifice all in the name of a great historical cause is exposed by the opposing con-viction that no cause is worth achieving in which individual human beings cease to count. It was the force of that principle that eventually shattered the military power and exhausted the political will of the totalitarian states. The triumph of the princi-ple of liberty, which is the other side of the modern world, has not arisen by accident. The conflict with the totalitarian foe would not have succeeded if it had not been rooted in the move-ment toward transcendent reality. Liberty is not an empty vessel into which we may place anything we choose. It is primarily an openness toward transcendent Being that cannot be contained within any mundane limits. This is why it could prevail in the contest with ruthless nihilist ideology.

The core of liberal political order is the transcendent finality of the individual, which it intuits without explicitly articulating. That is both the source of the endemic confusion and of the surprising resilience of liberal democratic politics. Without a clear identification of the direction that ultimately guides and justifies its orientation, liberal political thought is prone to endless vacillations. Is liberty indeed directed toward some ultimately serious end? Can it be just as well exercised through irresponsibility and dissipation? Is there or is there not one highest good toward which all are directed? The answer to all of these questions consists in the recognition that the end of liberty is transcendent, lying beyond all boundaries and definitions. There is no clear or single goal because no immanent or mundane good is capable of answering the purpose of liberty. The transcendent character of its goal defies all specification. That may render the conception and exercise of liberty a matter of enduring uncertainty, but it also preserves it from the deformation of all false absolutes. Silence concerning the end of liberty is the only appropriate way of representing its transcendent finality.

Rights Talk

The vagueness and vacuousness of the liberal political tradition is paradoxically both its weakness and its strength. We cannot gain much insight into the reality that sustains it by focusing only on the abbreviated statements of principle it supplies. Declarations of universal rights cursorily supported by the language of contractual agreement, constitutional limitations, and adumbrations of bonds of trust and solidarity are not enough. They are capable of interpretation in widely divergent directions. We are familiar with the incommensurable and interminable disputes that seem to increasingly fracture liberal societies. Culture wars and moral stridency seem ever more in evidence, and we are familiar with the inability of human rights documents to resolve international disputes. It is no wonder that many thoughtful observers have despaired entirely of the liberal language ever being rendered into any coherent form. Following the cue of Humpty Dumpty, its words seem to mean whatever we want them to mean. The compressed character of the liberal formulae provide little guidance in resolving disagreement over priorities among rights. Even the background of mutual responsibilities that is indispensable to sustaining an order of rights virtually disappears from public consciousness.

Clearly the success of a liberal political order, as attested by its durability over time, cannot be attributed to the clarity and coherence of its formulations. If we are to understand what sustains liberal politics, we must look much more at the substantive presuppositions of its practice. It is not what they say that explains liberal societies, but what they do. We must be willing to discern the animating convictions that guide the practice and even preserve liberal politics from the anarchy that seems to prevail in its theory. What is the source of its resonance, that sense of self-evident rightness that is satisfied with the most cursory explications of principle? At its core liberal politics is animated by the conviction of the inexhaustible depth of each individual human being. Everything we know about a particular individual can be enumerated and quantified. The sum of his or her contributions and costs can be calculated. Yet we know that we will never reach the totality of the person. No matter how well we know someone or how much he or she seems contained by the categories of our analysis, there always and inevitably remains an indecipherable abyss of mystery. It is as inexhaustible to the person himself or herself as to everyone else. That is the core recognition that resonates through the liberal political tradition. We respond to it because we recognize the truth of its valuation of the individual as an abyss of mystery beyond all finite measurement.

We sense that this is how it is appropriate to treat human beings. Any other frame of reference that sought to quantify them in terms of some finite scale would end by destroying everything of value in human life. All that is precious, all that constitutes the core of meaning for us, would be lost if we placed a limit on the dignity of human beings. Neither friendship nor love could survive the imposition of conditions on what we owe one another. Once we began to think in terms of one another as reaching a point where our usefulness had been exhausted, the point where we became dispensable in the name of some social whole, then we would cease to relate to one another in human terms. It is of the essence of human relationships that we recognize the unlimited and inviolable worth of each one. They cannot be weighed against one another. They never lose the status of ends in themselves, becoming reducible to the level of a mere means to some other good. There is no good higher than the good of a single individual human being. He or she outweighs the whole universe.

It is because the politics of liberty conveys that sense of the transcendent dignity of each one of us that it has such astonishing strength. Contrary to the squabbling surface exhibited by liberal societies, their deeper inspiration is profound. The power of their appeal arises from the degree of resonance with the most compelling perspective on human life. No more exalted conception of human beings can be provided. It may be that the liberal tradition is not particularly good at articulating the relationship to transcendent reality that brings human dignity into focus. That may require an expansion of the meditation into the revelatory experiences and symbols we have contemplated. But the liberal tradition is surprisingly effective at evoking that transcendent resonance indirectly through the valuation it implies about human beings. One is drawn from the liberal exaltation of transcendent individual dignity and worth toward the reality of transcendent Being itself. By contemplating the awesome dignity of the individual, we are drawn toward the source of that reverence in divine being.

Depth below Surface

A liberal political order is thus not a half-way house on the road toward nihilism. This recurrent misconception in the twentieth century has deflected attention away from the real challenge. It has discouraged the effort to deepen and solidify the liberal political order that is the only viable political form in the contemporary world. Thinking that liberal politics is merely the superficiality of rights talk, many critics have despaired of finding a means of remediating it. But there is more to the liberal political tradition than the face of anarchic self-indulgence that it so often presents to the world. Even the historic failure of liberal regimes, both in the Russian Revolution and in Weimar Germany, cannot be taken as representative cases. The fact that these two weak liberal democracies spawned the worst totalitarian regimes of the century cannot be regarded as the inevitable fate of liberal constitutional politics. Both regimes were in fact defeated by the combined resistance of the liberal democratic West and have now been replaced by such regimes themselves. For all their apparent inconstancy, there is a formidable strength within the liberal political tradition that cannot simply be dismissed—at least not until we have a more substantial possibility of discovering a replacement.

It is not enough simply to select certain patterns within liberal politics and extrapolate them toward their logical conclusion. This is an approach favored by conservative critics who see the epidemic of social disorder, everything from skyrocketing crimes rates to the soaring number of illegitimate births, and extend the process to the final and total collapse of order. They regard such phenomena as symptomatic of an inner flaw within the social and political tradition itself. Liberal democratic politics, they contend, gives exaggerated prominence to the notion of rights without sufficient counterbalancing attention to responsibilities. It encourages the unlimited assertion of rights without any constraining discipline of duties. Such a society cannot teach the virtues indispensable to its self-preservation. Eventually the process will have run so far that we will cease to recognize any common order or interest between us. Politics will have reverted to the naked contest of self-assertive wills. Without either the incentive to moderate our individual interests or the means of rationally resolving conflicts between them, nothing is left but the raw exercise of power. That apocalyptic vision of liberal democratic politics as "civil war carried on by other means" is what has galvanized the conservative appeal in reforming and restraining a process widely viewed as dangerously derailed.

The mistake, however, consists in attributing the blame to the inevitably corrosive tendency of liberal convictions. What such critics fail to recognize is that they too share such convictions and that their very reform efforts are intended to preserve the tradition of liberty, not eliminate it. The confusion is evident in the language itself. Progressive advocates of expanded individual rights are labeled "liberals," while their conservative opponents understand themselves as the preservers of liberty in the face of anarchy. The extent to which all sides revolve around the issue of free self-responsibility should alert us to the reality that they represent poles of the tension within the liberal tradition. Neither side is outside of the tradition, and what they do works to preserve it. Just as the New Deal/Great Society era was inaugurated to protect the sphere of individual liberty from social and economic forces that threatened it, the conservative reform of the welfare state arises from the same desire to invigorate the moral purpose of liberty. The reason why liberal democratic politics does not unravel into oppression or anarchy is that it continues to make such vital adjustments to changing circumstances. Conservative warnings would have been correct if there had been no conservative movement, just as progressives would have been correct in their warning if they had not succeeded in their reforms.

In each case the mistake has been to confuse the surface of liberal politics with its reality. Critics from the right or from the left have often tended to assume that they themselves were outside of the regime they were critiquing. They failed to realize that they were themselves one of the most central components of its self-remediation. The extent to which liberal political order embraces a considerable range of perspectives is indicative of its real strength. With the exception of the revolutionary extremes, all sides wish to see an order of liberty preserved. No substantive proposals for radical constitutional changes are advanced. Many suggestions are made for modifications, but they all lie within the continuum of the fundamental rightness of a rule of law respecting inalienable rights. The moral authority of liberal democracy now reigns unquestioned throughout the world. Even regimes that are neither liberal nor democratic feel compelled to dress themselves in the trappings of a liberal democracy. To a very considerable extent the disputes we encounter within both domestic and international politics are all disputes within a liberal framework. That supremacy of the liberal self-understanding is a powerful testament to the response it evokes within human beings. It is clearly not the house of cards liberalism is often assumed to be.

Even the debate about the shortcomings and defects of liberal politics must ultimately be conducted within liberal terms. This is the definitive proof of the primacy it occupies. We cannot conceive of any more penetrating analysis of the crucial issues than the liberal language of fundamental rights. When it comes to specific controversies, whether euthanasia, abortion, pornography, affirmative action, or anything else, it is only the arguments concerning the propriety of rights that decide the issue. We are not strongly taken by considerations of divine law or of moral imperatives. It is the appeal to the appropriate notions of fundamental rights that is ultimately decisive. Our whole notion of what is fair or just is bound up with the sense of the equal right of all human beings to equal respect and dignity. The inviolability of individual life and liberty is the turning point. Arguments that succeed in advancing that fundamental orientation invariably win the day. Theological and moral perspectives are tested by how far they advance or retard respect for human rights. There is no more compelling touchstone of what is right. The monopoly of moral authority exercised by liberal principles is revealed in the extent to which even religious leaders make their case in terms of promoting the fullest reverence for the person.

Consensus on Essentials

Once we begin to see the liberal political tradition as a powerfully compressed expression of a transcendent conviction, then we begin to understand the source of its strength. It has a capacity to resonate across a wide spectrum of controversies. By trusting to the transcendent truth embedded within liberal principles we can follow its intimations into the resolution of the most divisive conflicts that beset us. That may seem a rather optimistic claim, especially given the range and intensity of debates we encounter today. But the presence of debate is itself testament to the shared sense that a resolution is possible by reference back to the common convictions we share. Each side still holds onto the possibility of convincing its opponents. The real danger occurs when people walk away in despair from the conversation. That is when the shooting is likely to begin, not when they are remonstrating with one another. It is those who counsel silence, the smothering of controversy, who constitute the real danger.

So long as debate continues both sides share the conviction that the question cannot be settled until it is settled rightly. That is, they have a sense of a rightness to which they must appeal. Its core lies within the liberal principles whose consequences each side struggles to unfold as the means of making its case persuasive. The preeminent example of this kind of struggle must surely be the historical one of Lincoln and the slavery crisis. What is striking about Lincoln's approach to the debate is the confidence he had that a resolution could ultimately be attained through an expansion of the consequences for a free political order. The dispute did indeed oppose two liberal principles, democratic freedom of choice in the states and the equal rights of all human beings. On its surface it was an irresolvable difference, but Lincoln was confident of the inner coherence of the liberal political order. Its principles could not be in conflict. He set out to persuade his countrymen that the democratic self-government they professed to respect would itself be undermined by the refusal to acknowledge the equal rights of all human beings. It would lead directly to the implication that some have a right to rule over and enjoy the work of others. Slave owning was simply incompatible with a regime of liberty. It was the shared fundamental conviction to which he appealed that enabled him, even in the midst of civil war, to regard the division as destined to be reconciled.

It is when it is tested by the necessity of struggle against oppression that the inner strength of the liberal tradition emerges from its compressed depths. Tyrants from Hitler to Saddam Hussein have perennially miscalculated its apparent weakness. Of greater significance, however, is the tendency for liberal societies themselves to be deceived by the slackness of their order and the suspicion that deep down there is nothing deep down. Liberty is like the experience of transcendent Being that underpins it. Neither are cashable deposits that can be withdrawn from the bank at will. Rather it is a case of the account growing in strength and substance the more it is drawn into actuality. The result is that we apprehend the full measure and significance of liberty only as we are called upon to exercise it in defense of what is of transcendent value. By exerting ourselves in pursuit of what is highest we discover both the indispensable value of liberty and our participation in a reality beyond life itself. We are free because we are open to the word of truth that outweighs the whole world. The discovery surprises even ourselves.

From the perspective of that enlargement of our souls we can reflect more clearly on the nature of a liberal political order. We can recognize more clearly the kind of abridgement it involves. Liberal formulations of rights, consent, and rule of law are a way of condensing the long meditative articulation by which its existential sources are unfolded. It is a way of narrowing the public consensus to the points of essential agreement within a pluralistic social setting. This is the origin of the liberal formulations as they reached a recognizable identity in the seventeenth century. John Locke is the preeminent exemplar, as he provided the formulation of liberal democracy that justified the events of the Glorious Revolution of 1688. He provided the authoritative account of the source of government in the consent of individuals who compose civil society. They are each given by God the authority to rule themselves in accordance with their individual conceptions of the moral law but, as a result of the inevitable disagreements that will arise between men, consent to be ruled by the laws of civil society that they themselves have made. Government is thus instituted to protect the rights of life, liberty, and property that are the means by which each individual exercises responsible self-direction. The limitations imposed by government on each of us are only the minimum required to facilitate a life of freedom. There is little role for government in the broader formation or direction of the spiritual life of the citizens.

The summary essence of a liberal political order, which has remained fairly stable up to the present, sounds astonishingly spare. Generations of liberal thinkers have themselves wondered if their construction contained enough in the way of a substantive core to hold it all together. Was it, for example, merely an arrangement of convenience destined to come asunder as soon as individuals no longer found their interests served by it? How was it possible for governments to promote even the minimum virtues required to sustain their order, if they could no longer play a formative role in moral and spiritual affairs? How could we be sure that individuals would not misuse the power, especially the power of the majority, to extort and burden members of minority factions? If they entered into a contract to create society, what was to prevent them from contracting to commit injustice? What indeed was to preserve fidelity to their word so that they would not simply cut and run at the first sound of trouble? Clearly, a great deal more needed to be said about the foundations of liberal democracy. It was particularly necessary to find a way of connecting the essential public principles with broader moral and spiritual sources that alone could justify and animate their application.

The liberal concentration on the core elements of self-government was a brilliant solution to the problem of pluralism. The religious fragmentation of the early modern period had precipitated a political crisis as profound as any we have historically known. Indeed, we often fail to appreciate the depth of the cleavages opened by the collapse of the authority of the Church. Our own pluralist conflicts are by no means more radical, and we enjoy the inestimable advantage of a model of successfully resolving the divergences. Liberal democracy worked as a means of containing conflict because it relegated most such disputes to a private realm. Agreement was limited to the principles indispensable for lawful self-government. That provided a way for men and women of different theological convictions to remain faithful Christians without having to kill one another. Tolerance was possible within the framework of agreement on the essential political principles. But both tolerance and pluralism, while broad and destined to become broader, must always acknowledge their own limits. In the final analysis tolerance cannot be extended to the intolerant, those who wish to work for the destruction of the agreement that keeps the peace.

The need to sustain the convictions behind the liberal construction itself has become the major challenge. It is never merely enough to formulate the principles, for no contract can stand on its own. It must always be backed by the inner conviction of its rightness or fairness if it is to be sustained. The history of liberal political thought is largely the history of the efforts to make the justification for its order transparent. By persuasively articulating the rightness of the liberal construction we will have found a means of educating ourselves in the virtues that sustain the order we enjoy. Of course, the task of finding a compelling justification was rendered enormously difficult by the condition that the explanation must share the same neutrality as the liberal principles themselves. If it was to be a publicly available justification, then it could not reach into the vexed sphere of theological and philosophical questions that the liberal consensus had sought to avoid. Needless to say, the experiment has not been an overwhelming success.

Even thinkers of the genius of David Hume, Jean-Jacques Rousseau, Immanuel Kant, Georg Hegel, and John Stuart Mill have been unable to satisfy the critics of their interpretations. What is indeed striking about the whole project is the sheer diversity of justifications provided and the inability of any of them to win enduring consent. The problem is one that continues all the way up to the present. In our own time, John Rawls has attempted such a comprehensive *Theory of Justice* (1971) to underpin a liberal constitutional order. Now a quarter of a century later even he has largely abandoned the effort as a failure. The prevailing wisdom is that the task was impossible and that a liberal political order is merely the accidental fruit of a fortuitous historical convergence. It can have no theoretical defense because either such defenses are impossible or they are impossible under the limitations imposed by the requirements of a liberal society. The problem of liberal meaning parallels the broader crisis of meaning in the postmodern age, but it leads to more immediate practical consequences. If we cannot explain to ourselves why a liberal order of rights is worth preserving, it will not be possible for us to persuade ourselves and our children to retain it much longer. The theoretical crisis is reflected in a social crisis.

It is no wonder that the nature of the liberal democratic consensus is the number one subject of philosophical discussion. Discussions and books proliferate, continuing a rich historical pattern of reflection, because none has succeeded in defining its core. Why is it that a political arrangement of such worldwide popularity, and with such a demonstrable record of success, should be so uncertain of its justification? Why is liberal democracy unable even to explain itself to itself? Once we get beyond the level of political generalities about freedom, self-responsibility, and human dignity we find ourselves tongue-tied. The reason is, of course, not hard to find, as many contemporary observers have concluded. Departure from the most general formulae requires us to acknowledge that a liberal order is not neutral between competing moralities. Sure, the point of the liberal construction is to maximize individual freedom. But even that core cannot be articulated without presupposing some view of the human good toward which freedom must be exercised. What is the point of freedom if it does not enable us to realize what is good? That unfortunately is the question on which the whole liberal consensus comes apart.

The point of the liberal abbreviations of rights and liberty, we recall, was to remain silent about the different worldviews we regarded as important. Controversy was to be removed from the public arena and corralled safely within the private domain of individual choice. What was significant and what was compelling was up to us individually to decide. Public space was to be constituted by the purely formal arrangements that made this maximal exercise of private freedom possible. Constitutional and legal arrangements were to be value-neutral with respect to varying assessments of the human good. These were the sources of pluralism, of the social fragmentation that went all the way back to the theological cleavages that fractured the early modern period. Our disagreements have not lessened. How, then, can the liberal center hold if the divergences have invaded even its appearance of neutrality?

Transcendent Dignity of Person

The challenge is considerable but not insuperable. Most immediately we can admit that the game of neutrality is up. Liberal democracy is not neutral with respect to all conceptions of the good, only in relation to a certain range of moral and religious disagreements. It presupposes a more embracing moral order that the respective traditions within it are capable of recognizing. Among these are the convictions that human life is precious, that personal freedom is to be respected as the means by which individual responsibility is developed, and that ultimately it is the struggle to live in accordance with the moral intimations within us that constitutes the highest life for human beings. But how can we articulate this sustaining background to a liberal order without jeopardizing the peace between divergent philosophies? That is the nub of the difficulty. Clearly the answer does not lie in the direction of uncovering some ultimately neutral formulation without any presuppositions.

That is the rock on which all of our contemporary philosophical hopes have foundered. We never get beyond presuppositions. This is the limitation of our condition: we are already embedded in positions before our philosophizing begins. From another perspective, this is also our liberation, for we are relieved of the burden of the quest for the presuppositionless beginning. Instead we can begin where we are, immersed in a reality already structured by the pull of a mysterious meaning of which we are in search.

Respect for inalienable individual liberty embodies that transcendent openness as its political expression. Even more, it resonates with the experience of human beings who may have very varied capacities or inclinations to make their transcendent finality explicit. In other words, it evokes a practical response long before it wins theoretical approval. That is why liberal democratic politics has been such a runaway success. It does not depend on convincing people in principle of its rightness. They sense its appropriateness through its continuity with the never ending unfolding of their own experience. Within the context of that practical resonance all discussion of presuppositions and arguments pales into insignificance. The appeal of a liberal order is primarily existential.

It has long been recognized that the practice of self-government is the principal means of inculcating the virtues that make self-government possible. This was Tocqueville's major insight into the importance of the associational life of society as well as of the American federal arrangement. Through the dangerous exercise of liberty, he remarked, Americans had found a way of obviating those dangers. Nor is this insight lost in the contemporary scene. Within the awareness of the limited moral resources available to government there is a clear perception that one of the few effective means available is to encourage the exercise of self-responsibility. Governmental initiatives may waste more than financial reserves; they may drain the moral initiative of society. The Tocquevillian insight into the indispensability of individual exercise of self-responsibility now occupies the center of our attention. We cannot afford to jeopardize the dignity and self-worth attained only through liberty itself.

What is less well recognized are the existential dynamics involved in taking up that challenge. When we freely bend our efforts to promote our common good it is not simply that we more efficiently accomplish our goals. We actually become different.

The effort is one that has its greatest effect on the persons involved rather than on the policies enacted. Tocqueville alludes to without dwelling on the enlargement of soul that takes place in the strenuous exercise of liberty. It is a topic that deserves much more attention than political commentators are willing or able to give it. The change effected is not merely incidental or peripheral. In fact, it is central to the whole project of a self-governing society, for it brings into view the clear intuition of the enduring realities toward which the whole arrangement is constructed. Even without naming the transcendent goal, the straining of our efforts toward what is good and right renders the whole justification of liberty transparent. We see clearly what was only dimly intimated at the beginning: that human beings are made to stretch their efforts toward what is independently good, that this is the higher life toward which we are called and the route toward our participation in a reality that transcends all others. Liberty and choice are no longer empty words once we have acquired a concrete sense of the direction in which they must be unfolded.

Such a growth of the soul occurs without philosophical articulation. It later comes to recognize philosophical formulations as more or less adequate accounts of its immediate convictions, but it does not in any way depend on the validity of such justifications. That is the secret of the liberal constructions. Its philosophical abridgements have been just sufficient to call forth the resonances required to undertake the adventure of liberty. Once the process is initiated, it reveals a dynamic of its own that carries us forward toward heights of self-realization we could only dimly intuit in the abstractions with which we began. For this reason the inadequacies of the theoretical elaborations appear as incidental to the living movement of growth toward which they point. They can be accepted as approximations rather than as blueprints because the existential movement does not depend on their guidance. It is enough that they are available to give the enlargement of feeling and intelligence some fixity of definition. Theoretical articulations are necessary if the experience is not to dissipate into forgetfulness. There will be a recurrent need to resuscitate it. But that is a far cry from insisting that the theoretical difficulties must be resolved in advance or as the condition of engaging in moral growth.

Within this light the evident historical failure of the liberal political tradition to provide a coherent self-articulation must be regarded differently. It is no longer a failure. Now it must be viewed as part of the broader process by which a liberal political order recurrently awakens consciousness of the reality that draws it. The search for foundations is the theoretical counterpart of the existential practice of liberty. Despite the failure to reach any fully satisfactory account of foundations, the effort to do so keeps the consciousness of foundation alive. It is not a futile exercise. On the contrary, the rich history of liberal philosophical reflection from the seventeenth century up to the present is testament to the enduring character of the search in which it is involved. If it were fruitless, then there would be nothing to sustain it. In contrast, each generation begins with the same faith in the goal for which it seeks and struggles to explain its inspiration to itself. The fact that none of the accounts becomes definitive does not signify failure. In each of them living contact is made with the source of the movement that underpins them. By straining toward the transcendence out of reach we gain a greater sense of its reality.

It is at this point that the appropriateness of liberal incompleteness and tentativeness becomes clear. How else can the transcendent goal of human existence be represented except through the consciousness of our failure to represent it? Liberal silence about ultimate reality may now no longer be viewed as a regrettable failure of consensus and articulation, but as its great theoretical contribution. Far from being an absence of meaning, it can now be seen as arising from a fullness of meaning that transcends all symbolization. The insistence of many liberal thinkers that there is no highest good in terms of which all other goods must be ranked and that the liberal toleration of diversity reflects this irreducible plurality must be viewed in this sense. It arises from the conviction that any highest good, once it is named, becomes suspect as an illegitimate contraction of the full reach of the human spirit. The latter can only be answered by a good that transcends all names. But whence comes that conviction if not from the living sense of its presence? Liberal silence about the transcendent is the one that pays its respect most profoundly.

To avoid the other danger of lapsing from silence into forget-fulness, however, it is necessary to keep the struggle toward artic-ulation alive. Both the practical and theoretical reaching of a lib-eral political tradition are the indispensable means by which we actualize the resonances it contains. The incompleteness and pro-visionality of all attainments is not the last word. Liberal political practice and reflection is simply a way in which we work out our participation in the meaning of the mystery that guards all of human life. The appropriateness of liberal evocations must be as-sessed within this context. Only then does it become apparent that two correlative processes are at work within the liberal con-struction. There is first the concentration on the consensus nec-essary for moral and political order. Much of the resonance nec-essary for sustaining this consensus is preserved in the silence respectfully observed before the transcendent mystery of the goal of human life. That resonance, we have seen, cannot be ade-quately articulated, but it can be evoked through the practice and reflection in which it is pursued.

Dignity as Moral Advance

The second process at work in this liberal concentration on es-sentials is a heightening of awareness of the transcendent moral worth of each individual. This is perhaps the most overlooked dimension in the contemporary preoccupation with our short-comings. But it is the key both to the inexorable moral pressure within liberal societies and to the inescapable tendency to debate moral issues within liberal terms. Human rights are not just a shorthand for the moral code of our relationships to one another. They also direct a spotlight on the central dimension of respect for the inner person that ultimately is at the core of our moral convictions. Any proposed moral order that fails to enhance the inviolable dignity of each person cannot stand before the liberal scrutiny directed at it. Liberal order heightens our sensitivity to that inescapable dimension. The point of all moral and political conventions, we have learned, is to enable the inner growth of the person toward the goal that is beyond all finite characterizations. Any preimposed limitations on the full dynamic of the human soul can no longer defend its legitimacy.

We see this dynamic working itself out in the moral controversies that widely beset us today. Invariably the most powerful arguments on either side of the abortion, euthanasia, genetic and behavioral engineering, affirmative action, and capital punishment debates are all derived from the core of the liberal conception of rights. Despite the confusion that also prevails in the use and misuse of the liberal vocabulary, we cannot afford to forget that these issues are being fought out largely in liberal terms. And that is so not simply because such terms are the only publicly available medium of discourse. It is much more because they are the most morally authoritative formulations we have. A liberal tradition heightens our awareness of the moral dimensions of human relationships that cannot be jeopardized. It focuses our attention on what is of transcendent importance, that which cannot be lost without losing everything. We recognize that what is at stake in each of these issues is not just the rightness or wrongness of a particular action, but the whole way we understand who we are and how we treat one another. If we fail to respect the fundamental reality of the person in one of these instances, then it calls into question the seriousness of our commitment in all others. Nothing is more important than the irrefragable dignity of the person.

Euthanasia, for example, is presented to us as an issue in which the freedom of self-determination is at issue. Does it not enhance the dignity of human life to be free to choose the time and manner of our departure from it? What could be more inhumane than to refuse the relief of suffering to those in the terminal stages of an illness? One of the reasons why voluntary euthanasia has made such headway is that it seems to appeal directly to the same liberal sentiments. All that seems to matter is that we take care to ensure that the necessary safeguards against abuse are followed. So long as a truly informed consent has been given, we need have no scruples about accommodating the wishes of the terminally ill. It is only when we reflect on the consequences in practice that the darkness contained in the suggestion becomes evident. Voluntary euthanasia means that some human beings will be deciding who will live and who will die. Surely we will exercise some discrimination among those who request the services of euthanasia professionals. How will they in turn make that decision?

They can make it in the only way that any of us would. We will have to decide which lives still have some sustaining merit and which are no longer worth preserving. Even if the patient has already decided that his or her quality of life has slipped below an acceptable level, we cannot avoid entering into the same judgment if we are to facilitate their wishes. What criteria will we use? We can think of none that do not involve a process of measuring and weighing the value of human life. We will inevitably be involved in the process of defining what a person is worth. What pain or inconvenience costs too much? We can no longer use the standard of every person as an end-in-himself or herself, since they must now be assessed in terms of their aggregate contribution to themselves or others. The euthanasia situation compels such a finite reduction of the value of human life.

Once we have entered into that process we cannot appeal to safeguards to prevent abuse. Now we will recognize that the limits we impose on the practice are entirely our own. There are no longer any absolute barriers on the way in which we can treat one another. The only barriers that exist are ones that we have chosen to adopt. We might shift to different criteria, and inevitably different people will interpret the different criteria differently. Some will err on the side of life, some on the side of death. Either way we will have no way of distinguishing the abusive from the non-abusive because there are no fixed limits. We cannot say when evil has occurred. It is only then that we realize the abyss opened up by the euthanasia suggestion. The extension of the liberal practice of rights to the very parameters of human existence itself does not constitute a true expansion of liberty. It opens up the loss of all rights if our fate is to be decided by other human beings determining who will live and who will die, based on nothing more than their own subjective goodwill. We have lost all rights if there are no fixed limits. Once everything becomes a matter of choice we have become totally subject to the whim of others. They are the ones who decide the limits since none are already pregiven.

What is interesting about this argument is that it reaches its conclusion without appealing to any larger theological or philosophical presuppositions. It has emerged from within the liberal framework itself. Strongly resonant, of course, is the opening toward a transcendent order beyond human life, and it no doubt appeals most to those who are in touch with more robust and explicit spiritual traditions. Behind the liberal debates larger conflicts of spiritual orientation are being worked out. Clearly, the deepest resonance of those who support euthanasia is the rebellious spirit of human self-assertion. It is the secular mentality that wants to dominate reality independently. Opposing it is the countervailing submission to an order whose source lies mysteriously beyond us. That is the attitude of trust in the goodness of the cosmos in which we find ourselves. But the debate itself can be fought out in largely, if not strictly, liberal terms. This is because the liberal language of rights is both a compressed expression of what can be more elaborately unfolded as the transcendent openness of human nature and because it represents a moral heightening of the core moral issues within that orientation. That is why we can have faith in the eventual resolution of the debates.

Just as Lincoln observed of the slavery crisis, conflicts over rights cannot be settled until they are resolved rightly. Permanent incorporation of any settlement less than the morally appropriate one would cause too much of a disruption to the whole liberal framework. Such controversies will continue inexorably under their own internal moral pressure toward a resolution. In their refusal to go away we see perhaps one of the most significant dimensions of the heightening of moral consciousness involved in the liberal concentrations. There is simply no way to avoid the recognition that the elimination of the rights of one group or one area of life infects with uncertainty the whole structure of rights everywhere. If it is a matter of governmental or popular determination in one case, why not in all others? An order of rights is too deeply embedded in the transcendent order of reality for it to be swept aside by the prevailing pressures of convenience and confusion. Such deformations do and will occur, but they cannot get a permanent foothold within the authoritative expression of what is right. The formidable strength of the language of rights is that it has, for all its peremptory compression of order, made the abuse of fundamental rights more difficult to sustain. One has only to look at the impressive use to which liberal moral language was put by the dissidents of the communist era.

At the same time we can never afford to forget that the authoritative account of order constitutes only a part of the publicly available world of meaning. By far the largest part is occupied by broader cultural issues. It is a grave mistake for politics to forget this larger cultural context within which its own struggle for order takes place. The literary, artistic, and philosophical debates between competing worldviews are worked out within the arena of civilizational meaning. Ultimately the liberal moral and political order depends on those wider resonances beyond itself. It is not enough to rely on the compressed illumination of the debates about rights to resolve the issues. A liberal order cannot stand alone. It depends on a wider context of spiritual traditions, intellectual vitality, and civilizational meaning that it cannot create. Even to say that liberal democracy is largely a secular expression of Christianity is not to say that it can be sustained without the presence of the more robust spirituality of the world religions. The heightened intensity of liberal public language is likely to become shrill, unbalanced, and confused if it is not sustained by the kind of broader faith in a transcendent order of grace and forgiveness represented by the revelatory traditions. That is why the question of cultural meaning, the effectiveness of the appeals of cultural movements, cannot be a matter of indifference from a political perspective. It is within the cultural arena that the life and death of a civilization is largely determined.

CHAPTER 7

CULTURAL TRANSPARENCE

T HE INTENSE but narrow beam of liberal political principles cannot constitute the meaning of a civilization.
There are simply too many questions left unaddressed.
Despite the dramatic illumination cast by the recognition of the
incomparable worth and depth of each individual, its authoritative truth cannot stand alone. Even for its recognition, we have
seen, it depends on the acknowledgment of the larger mystery in
which we participate. Somewhere that rich web of relationships
must be explored. Politics is a field in which too much is at stake
to permit the unfettered explorations of the spirit. Instead, the
free competition of ideas and symbols must take place in an
arena in which the consequences do not place the very survival of
order in jeopardy. There is no impermeable barrier between the
worlds of culture and politics but there is a zone of separation. It
is true that poets are an alternative legislature, but their writings
do not immediately have the force of law. Lacking command of
an army, their power must be derived directly from the spiritual
truth of their appeal. The cultural free marketplace of ideas and
symbols is the arena in which the quest for meaning is pursued
most openly.

In many ways this is the culmination of the meditation we

have been following. The test of what we have discovered about the sources of meaning is whether they can evoke an answering response in the public realm. Can they constitute the meaning of a civilization? This chapter is not an afterthought appended to round out the reflection on meaning with a cultural component. It should rather be read as arising from all that has preceded. The sense of the end of the modern experiment in creating a man-made world with its finite boundary of meaning and fulfillment forms the background. Within that context we have discovered the openness to transcendent mystery as the dynamic center of meaning in existence. Neither our freedom nor the directions we pursue can be sustained without it. We are an unlimited aspiration drawn inescapably toward a reality beyond all that we can know. That is the mystery constituting the silent boundary of our lives. From time to time illuminative glimpses of its divinity are vouchsafed to us and we recognize ourselves in the historically transmitted traditions. Now we must ask, Can this tentative intimation of meaning expand into a publicly symbolized whole? Can postmodern civilization become transparent for the mystery that draws it beyond itself?

In an important sense the answer is that it already has, although that recognition has perhaps yet to be made. We often labor under the impression of the modern world as irrevocably fragmented. It appears to be a dizzying succession of cultural movements no one of which succeeds in imposing its form or identity for any continuing period of time. But that in itself is hardly sufficient reason to conclude that meaning has escaped us. The very vitality contained in the succession of creative efforts testifies to a faith in the goal that inspires them. It is only if we were tempted to give up the pursuit in despair that we would be entitled to conclude that the modern world constitutes nothing but a cultural wasteland. Ironically we may be closer to that moment of creative exhaustion today as a result of the cumulative sense of the end of the modern world. We are tempted to view its cultural and artistic disappointments in the same light: the death of meaning includes the death of art.

That, however, would be an unjustified extrapolation. Nothing is more evident than that modern art, literature, and music has constituted an impressive world of meaning. The instability of forms that has marked cultural experiments do not signify a collapse of meaning. In some respects they can be regarded as denoting a fullness of meaning that cannot be contained—at least not within the available forms. The sheer restless fecundity of movements and artists in the past two hundred years attests to a civilizational vitality that cannot be gainsaid. Each of them has succeeded within their own parameters of creating or evoking a world of meaning. One cannot think of a Joyce or an Eliot, a Mann or Mahler, a van Gogh or a Shostakovitch, and complain about the poor artistic heritage of the past one hundred years. The fact that none of them succeeded in imposing a stable form on the broader context does not imply that their efforts have failed to constitute a meaningful raid on the inarticulate mystery of existence. The transitory and provisional nature of their evocations does not necessarily denote futility; it can also represent a deeper realization of the ineffable mystery toward which they are directed. That is the turning point on which we are balanced as a civilization. On which side we fall will determine whether we will be able to find a means of publicly evoking the mystery of transcendent Being that constitutes meaning in existence.

Art as Openness to Being

Our lives are constituted by the tension drawing us toward the fullness that forms the horizon of our consciousness. The light of longing is what illumines the path before us, providing the whole vitality of interest and movement in our lives. It is an inescapably transcendent aspiration, for a succession of endlessly similar satisfactions would quickly exhaust their appeal. We have seen that it is the unlimited openness of our trajectory that underpins the character of our freedom. We are never what we are going to be and in that realization we are free. It is the same illumination that reveals the moral direction of our lives as we respond to the promptings of our hearts. Occasionally and unmeritedly the horizon of mystery silently drawing us opens to reveal its loving depth and we are touched by grace. But we are not permitted to live permanently in that luminous presence. The door closes again and we must struggle to draw forth its implications for the moral and political principles by which we must live. A broader effort to constitute meaning requires us to search for the imaginative symbols and forms in which such eruptions can be given evocative permanence. That larger cultural enterprise is the collaborative effort of many human beings, not only the artistic elites. It is the fruit of the great continuing conversation between all of us that constitutes the world of cultural meaning.

Perhaps it is not surprising therefore to discover that it is not as drained of mystery and meaning as it is reputed to be. Our cultural self-understanding may not have the same substantive grasp on the symbols of spiritual illumination, it may no longer be a Christian civilization, but this does not mean that it is tone-deaf to the call of transcendent truth. Modern civilization is, as Flannery O'Connor said of the South, "Christ haunted." The memory of the Christian movement toward transfiguration may be all that is left, but that is not yet the same as the forgetfulness of Being against which Heidegger struggled so much. There is still recollection, and it can be stirred to life only because the embers of our own quest for transcendence remain a present reality. It is not a large distance toward the realization that the absence of transcendent symbols does not necessarily imply the disappearance of God. We recall that transcendent Being is what cannot be represented. The fullness for which we hunger is perhaps more intensely present in the absence than in all the apparently massive symbolizations of history. Within the meditative dynamics of the absence that is present we are perhaps not as far from the kingdom of God as we thought.

It is not surprising that the concrete explorations of artists, writers, and musicians should bring the underlying depth of the modern world to light. There is a striking contrast between the impoverishment and deformation of spirit within the revolutionary ideological movements and the human openness and depth that still prevails within the world of creative imagination. It is no accident that so many of the dissidents of the twentieth century have come from the world of art. Their own work puts them in touch with the unfathomable mystery of existence, and the contrast with the hollow instrumentalization of ideology could not be greater. No great art can be in the service of ideology. It can be in the service of religion because religion is rooted in the same inexhaustible openness. The one-dimensional stridency of ideology, vainly masquerading as the fullness of reality, cannot withstand the probing of artistic openness. As soon as an artist puts himself at the service of a closed political system he has sold his soul. Almost by definition, the vocation of the artist calls him to resist all closure of the openness to the horizon of mystery.

To be true to itself art must be true to the full interplay of forces within experience. Any peremptory closing off of avenues of experience is an impoverishment of the work of art. What makes the work of creative artists and, by extension all of us who engage in the responsive unfolding of imagination, so important is that it is a primary vehicle for exploring the mystery of reality within which we find ourselves. Art, like life, is a response to the pulls that impinge upon us and by responding to art we enter more deeply into the reality that draws us. We are on the way toward revelation, that piercing of the veil of mystery in which we obtain a glimpse of the whole. It is not a process of reasoning, nor does it follow any predetermined pattern, but it does lead us toward a fuller understanding if we do not close ourselves off prematurely from the unfolding. We may not be able to explain what is going on in this concrete imaginative unfolding, but we can be sure that it draws us toward a fuller realization of the truth. The reason is that art, if it is faithful to itself, is a submission to the direction disclosed by reality itself.

Art is in the service of reality. It is a quest for truth, and what constitutes its beauty is that it makes the truth radiantly present in symbols, images, sounds, and embodiments. The greatness of art is precisely its unwavering fidelity to the truth disclosed by reality itself. It is through art that the truth of various positions are tested. They are brought into juxtaposition and we see what they are in the truth of "living life," as Dostoevsky termed it. His understanding of the role of the artist is in many ways paradigmatic. For Dostoevsky, art was great when the artist had virtually disappeared behind his creation. The characters had acquired a reality of their own. It was their voice that was given expression and the directions the characters pursued flowed naturally from who they are, not from any preconceived convictions of the artist. By submitting so completely to the demands of verisimilitude the writer, Dostoevsky knew, ran the risk of losing control of his creation. It might point toward conclusions with which he disagreed. But the inestimable merit of this openness was that the truth that emerged from the juxtapositions had the status of independence. Having been tested in the crucible of life, it had the authority of reality itself.

Such a radically open exploration of the plural intimations of experience is fraught with risk. There is no guarantee that it will be brought to a successful or even an acceptable conclusion. What if the anarchic freedom of art points toward sadism? If the pleasure of torturing the innocent is proclaimed as the highest truth about man, what can we say in response? When we contemplate the many opportunities for shipwreck on this voyage we are impressed by its lonely uncertain character. All we can say is that we must enter on the exploration in the spirit of trust that seems to be present from the beginning. We must rely on the reality that draws us, and believe that the dimensions of its mystery will reveal themselves in order to us. If we seem to be drawn toward what is unspeakably evil, then we must trust that the countervailing force of good will become even more manifest before us. In this sense it mirrors the odyssey of life. We can only engage in it if we are held fast by the confidence that if sin abounds grace abounds even more. There are many instances of artists who have perverted their gifts in order to advance their own megalomaniacal pride. Prometheanism is not by any means absent from the world of art, as the architectural schemes for mile-high buildings and for totally planned environments powerfully attest. All we can say is that they quickly encounter the limits of reality itself. The salvation of art is that it can never depart from the parameters of reality with which it is irrevocably and concretely engaged.

Art without Common Language

Perhaps the peculiar temptation to which art in the modern period is exposed arises from the unique position of the artist. Since the Renaissance artists have definitively shed their anonymity. Today they occupy positions of great social prominence and celebrity. They are exalted to a quasi-divine status because of what they do. No longer merely the servants of reality, they are also viewed as its creators. Men like Leonardo da Vinci were filled with the self-confidence that they possessed the means not only of imitating nature but of improving on it. It you look at his *Madonna of the Rocks* you will see what this means. No real-life Madonna ever had such translucent flesh and no stones ever contained such radiant depth. That pattern of regarding artists not only as discoverers but as creators of meaning continues up to recent times. For many, art becomes a religion, and we hear sufficient discussion of the capacity of art to evoke a spiritual awakening. That whole pattern is of course no accident. The new centrality of art begins at precisely the time when the spiritual coherence of Western civilization is becoming dislodged. In a time of growing uncertainty art holds out the promise of an authoritative transparence.

All that has changed in the later phase of this process is that artists can no longer look toward an inherited supply of symbols rooted in a more-or-less continuing spiritual consensus. The fracturing of meaning has continued beyond the Renaissance and the Reformation, such that the modern secular world that began in the eighteenth century exists without any transcendent frame of reference. Chaos is intensified as we witness the rise of secular messiahs in the nineteenth century and the secular religious movements of the twentieth-century mass ideologies. A limit is reached in Nietzsche's verdict on the age as defined by the nihilistic death of God. The anarchy of public meaning, which is tantamount to its collapse, defines the new context for art in the modern world. It now must make its way in splendid isolation from any broader communal self-understanding. In contrast to the artistic explorers of the Renaissance, who, for all their divergences, could still rely on a considerable body of inherited spiritual themes and symbols, the artists of the past two hundred years have had to create without any publicly available points of reference. Not only do they work alone but their works must be able to stand alone within the world.

That is the formidable context for art and cultural meaning in the modern period. It goes a long way toward explaining the multiplicity of styles and proliferating forms. Every artist has to invent his or her own style because no common forms are available or none have succeeded in attaching themselves to an enduring public consensus. The last successful artistic style in Western civilization was the baroque. Its enduring impact is still evident in the widespread presence of baroque churches, music, and paintings throughout Europe and Latin America. This stable form was briefly succeeded by a movement known as neoclassicism which harkened back to the models of the Renaissance and the classical world. That was already a largely imitative form that quickly wore itself out in slavish exaggeration. The enduring neoclassical monuments, evident in L'Enfant's Washington, D.C., or Jefferson's architectural achievements, derive their power from the classical resonances they contain. Only in the hands of a truly exceptional artist, such as Mozart, do they transcend the limitations of the form to include the deepest human explorations. As a formal approach the neoclassical movement could not be sustained in the hands of lesser artists and, in the final analysis, that is the true test of stylistic strength.

The pattern of artistic development in the modern era is already established. Great works continue to be produced by truly exceptional artists, but the formal means at their disposal must be left behind as the transitory shell of their achievements. Without formal continuity or stability, the modern era is marked by the distinctive illuminations of genius while an endless stream of mediocrities must be quickly forgotten. Greatness remains, but the average sinks to a new level of vacuity. This has much to do with the ugliness and tastelessness of the modern world, for the average person can have no stable conception of good form. Standards become the exclusive preserve of connoisseurs. Creatively it is only a great artist who is capable of rising to the challenge that defines the artistic context of the present. He or she must be capable of evoking an artistic meaning that transcends the formal means at their disposal. Their creation must be capable of enduring when their style has become obsolete.

Romantic Return to Experience

The search for a new artistic language in a world whose traditional symbols have become opaque was explicitly declared as the project of the romantics. That was the first occasion when the modern context of the artistic quest for meaning became self-conscious. The romantics occupy a position of prominence, not necessarily because of their achievements, but because of their perception of the challenge. It had now fallen to the artist to render the transcendent mystery of existence, restoring the transparence that had been lost when the inherited Christian forms had ceased to function. Romanticism is defined by its understanding that meaning can only be constituted by its tension toward transcendent being. Confined to a mundane rationality and a finite range of fulfillments, human life loses its significance. If religion can no longer provide the overarching meaning, there must be a replacement. Without that movement toward a fullness of reality beyond all that this world contains everything within this life is drained of meaning too. The romantics experienced the modern problematic with an intensity that has not been surpassed. That is why, although romanticism has been followed by many successor movements, it is the one that provides the arch of self-understanding within which they have unfolded. Art as the means of making contact with the mysterious beyond of all meaning is the preeminent romantic quest.

"Religions pass, but God remains," was a remark of Victor Hugo much favored by van Gogh. It expresses the faith that sustained the romantic quest when religion had failed them for, in an important sense, they had not failed religion. Rather, they saw themselves as keeping the faith alive when its institutional carriers had lost their inner life. Their faith had become detached from the revelatory traditions and now sought to clothe itself in more perspicuous forms. No hostility toward the Church or medieval Christianity was implied. On the contrary, they often harbored deep admiration for the historical traditions, but they also recognized the undeniable gap that distanced them from their predecessors. The symbols no longer or at least no longer immediately invited the opening toward transcendence that the romantics knew within their own hearts. To them had fallen the task of imaginatively unfolding the intimations of transcendence preserved nowhere else but within them. Like the remnant of Israel, they awaited a new rebirth of the spirit. What they least suspected was that the deepening of experience in which they engaged would eventually lead them back to the historically differentiated symbols as their most transparent account. Despairing of the traditional carriers, they discovered they had themselves become the historical medium.

This pattern is evident in the interiorization of experience that is at the core of the romantic project. Instead of looking toward the biblical or historical exemplars of spiritual experience, the romantics shifted their attention to the inner illumination itself. Symbolic and external trappings slipped away as they focused on unmediated experiences. Romantics seek not to present us with the heroic witnesses to truth but with truth itself. We are all to become direct participants in the luminous unfolding. It is art that now opens the door of encounter with transcendent Being. Requiring neither theological nor symbolic elaboration, the experience is presented with the full force of its immediacy. No one can be skeptical of its reality nor doubtful about its impact. By presenting the irresistible truth of experience the romantics were confident that they had themselves led the way toward a great spiritual awakening. No one could gainsay the overwhelming power of unmediated mystery itself.

That direct presentation of transcendent mystery was perhaps best accomplished in the paintings of Caspar David Friedrich. Their most striking quality is the sense of limitless sacred space they convey. Most of his scenes are outdoor in fields, on mountains, by the sea, but none of them invites the casual disportment of a picnic. Right away we are given the sense that we are in the presence of a mystery, a holiness that calls for the appropriate reverence. Friedrich's goal, which he shared with other romantics, is to evoke an immediate response of awe before the setting itself. There are no overtly supernatural events. Occasionally churches or crucifixes project from the landscape but they are firmly tied to this world. Transcendence is conveyed directly by the awe-inspiring abyss of space unfolded before us. Air and light are the primary carriers of mystery. All of this is brought together most famously in a painting entitled *A Monk by the Shore of the Sea*. Most of the picture consists of a vast expanse of sky; below, there is a narrow band of ocean and a similarly limited stretch of shore. Standing alone on the shore is the tiny figure distinguishable in his Capuchin habit. Nothing else exists; even a couple of far-off boats that were originally included by the artist were painted out in the final revision. The effect is powerful, for the viewer participates in the same numinous experience of the monk. There can be no mistake about the abyss of mystery before us.

The same intention that we should come away changed particularly underlies romantic poetry, but it is in the emotional directness of music that the project reaches its summit. Poetry and music are quintessentially romantic because of the immediacy of experience they convey. The primacy of experiential exploration is perhaps best revealed in Beethoven, whose music depicts heroic or pastoral events, but is much more concerned to convey them directly. Sacred music in the hands of Beethoven is no longer primarily about the sacred texts and rites it is designed to accompany. Now it has become a medium for exploring the inner spiritual struggles of the composer, his doubts and convictions, his suffering and redemption. This does not necessarily imply a downgrading of the central Christian events; rather, it is a new and more personal avenue into their meaning through the path of human experience. The height of Beethoven's art is surely the late string quartets in which he reveals the inner struggle of his soul most completely. There is especially the exploration of suffering in his last quartet, Opus 135, with its agonized question, Must it be so? and then finally the transformative grace of acceptance, It must be so. The compression of the mystery of existence, its raw penetration, could not proceed much further. We begin to see why this work remains a monument of the human spirit.

The great risk of the romantic emphasis on experience is that it might lose all reference to the reality beyond experience. In searching for the experience of God, they might come to believe only in the God of their experience. The temptation to idolize the experience itself is, of course, a long-standing danger of the mystical path. Eventually the obsession with experience does become the rock on which their project founders, but it would be grossly unfair to lay the blame at the feet of the great romantic pioneers. It is enough to note the ambivalence within their constructions. The problem is well illustrated in an important neglected oratorio of Franz Schubert. His *Lazarus* took up the gospel story of Christ's raising of Lazarus, except that Schubert's account ends with the death of Lazarus, not with his resurrection. Many interpreters have taken this change to indicate Schubert's loss of faith in resurrection or an afterlife, and have argued that it was a reduction of the gospel story to his own romantic preoccupation with the finality of death. But a more careful reading of the libretto and the music suggests the superficiality of this view. Schubert was not drawn toward the idea of Lazarus's resurrection because it would have constituted no more than a prolongation of this earthly life. His interest centered on the movement toward a higher life for which death itself was the door. That is the message of Christ, that Lazarus has already risen to the higher life in which he is one with God. His physical resurrection would only have been an obstacle to his final end. Admittedly, the double meaning of life is already present in the gospel story, but Schubert has separated them for the sake of preserving the higher. It testifies to the single-minded focus on the experience of transcendence that he was willing to surrender the symbol of life for the sake of reaching its reality.

In many respects this constitutes the limit of exploration. Once the experiences have been so deeply mined nothing further can be said, or at least there can be no further development in the direction of unfolding them more completely. The extent of the romantic achievement is one of the principal reasons why the romantics retain their perennial appeal and inspire periodic renewals all the way up to the present. Romanticism is the overriding arch of cultural movements for the past two hundred years. We cannot go any deeper into the experiences they brought to light; we can only repeat them without extending them. They are at the limits of the illumination vouchsafed to human beings. Of course, we have lost much of the naïveté of the early romantics, their blissful confidence in a dawning new age or their optimism about the power of art itself. But we cannot penetrate beyond the mystery of the all in which we find ourselves or reach higher than the miracle of love that draws us toward a higher life within. The romantic durability is drawn from the strength of experience itself.

Submission to Order

Yet the formidable spiritual opening of the romantics did not preclude the tendency to push its limits to the breaking point. The history of art in the postromantic era is largely the history of the disintegration of their evocations. In this sense they continue to dominate, to provide the overarching meaning, only now it is in the mode of fragmentation. The direction pursued by succeeding cultural movements may seem remote from the search for transcendent depth of romanticism but they would be inconceivable without that background. They are still in search of the same goal of contact with the unlimited, which they suspect lies just over the horizon depicted by the romantics. In this sense the rejection of romanticism is itself a romantic inspiration. The seeds were already present within the restless dynamic of the romantic era itself, the thrusting toward a mystery without limit. Combined with the free-floating quality of their inquiry, which occurred outside of all received interpretations and disciplines, it was perhaps inevitable that the authority of the romantics themselves would be challenged by the new pioneers of the spirit. The only constant remained the primacy of cultural leadership retained by the artist.

In music we can literally hear the disintegration of the romantic ethos. Perhaps it is because romantic influence proved so durable in that medium or because it particularly lends itself to the romantic quest. The break is exemplified in the career of Arnold Schoenberg whose *Transfigured Night*, a quintessentially romantic subject of a moonlight conversation between two deeply troubled lovers, pushes the harmonic possibilities to their limits. We recognize the overripe quality of late romanticism in this music and sense the extent to which the very lushness borders on a decadent indulgence for its own sake. Now the richness of possibilities for elaboration have become an obstacle rather than an avenue toward communication. The limits of reconciling dissonance have been reached in this overdeveloped language which luxuriates virtually under its own impetus. It is with a certain sense of relief that we witness the turn away from this dead end toward a more spiritually austere musical form. This is precisely what Schoenberg and his Viennese colleagues attempted with the much maligned twelve-tone or serial music. In place of use of the single tone or key dominance of previous music, they sought to explore the possibilities of each tone serially within a piece of music. The achievements of their approach were perhaps modest, although not negligible, but their example was profoundly influential. They showed that romanticism did not have to end in dissolute self-absorption. It could be saved through the discipline of submitting more rigorously to the demands of reality itself.

A similar search for discipline, structure, order is at work in other styles as well. The romantic absorption with experience is tempted to luxuriate in the experience as an end in itself. As a mystical way it is beset by the perennial danger of falling in love with the experience of God rather than with the God of experience. What could be more attractive than to remain on the mountain with the transfigured Lord? We are all inclined to build tabernacles of escape there. But then the meaning of the episodic nature of our access to transcendent mystery begins to disclose itself. Without the necessity of returning to the routine of everyday experience, we would eventually lose our hold on the reality that held us. By seeking to retain the experience, we are left only with our inner feelings, while the reality slips through our grasp. It is only if we are compelled to maintain our steadfast attention on the reality of transcendent Being, even when its experience is absent, that we can be sure of reaching its reality and not merely our experience of it. That is the hard lesson of romanticism, and it is one that has been explored concretely over the past century as artists have sought to work their way back to it. The starting point has been the recognition that the romantic aspiration for transcendent illuminations has overlooked the access provided by more immediate experiences of reality.

They retain, in other words, the core romantic faith that reality discloses itself to us even as they seek a more reliable means of illumination. Typical of this reaction is the movement known as realism. Instead of constructing a painting or writing a novel around the epiphany of meaning, such artists deliberately eschew moments of significance. They avoid privileged events and per-spectives in favor of casual cross sections of life. It is another form of the romantic faith which now pins its hope on the typi-cal, the ordinary, and the uncontrived. There, the expectation is, truth is to be found. Artists like Manet and Courbet and writers like Zola or Dickens went to considerable trouble to avoid the sense of deliberate construction behind their work. It was a snap-shot of reality, albeit a carefully designed nondesign of the world. For all the inner conflicts within this conception, they very often succeeded in disclosing the transcendent mystery of the ordinary in ways that the high-minded romantics could never conceive. This is particularly true of the unforgettable dignity revealed in the life and work of the humblest classes of society who had never before enjoyed a role in the history of art.

A similar faith in the capacity of the immediate dimensions of experience to lead us toward mystery is present even in move-ments so apparently absorbed with the surface. Impressionism is often disdained as such a superficial phenomenon, a reputation not helped by the enormous appeal it continues to exercise on the public imagination. It is easy to dismiss Monet's waterlilies, or Renoir's parasolled women, or Debussy's pianistic images, or Ravel's exoticism as spiritually trivial. They seem to be so im-mersed in the surface that no question of depth can arise. But the durability of their appeal belies the charge of sheer superficiality. They are certainly not glib. Granted they are concerned with the impressions, the appearances of things, but they present us not merely with an outer shell bereft of mystery. Rather, it is a surface shimmering with beauty, radiant in its own light. We notice that the tone of their works is indeed reverential. Appearance is being treated as a reality in its own right, one that if we can listen to or see it will reveal its own beauty to us. Illumination has been brought to or from the surface. Which is which is no longer of great matter.

The lightness of the approach has of course its own limitations. There are dimensions of experience that cannot be contained within the sunny appearance of things however radiant they may be. Inevitably impressionism is followed by more robust artistic forms that search more profoundly the inner reaches of the human spirit as it strains toward the starry heaven. This recalls the work of van Gogh who marks the breaking of the impressionist mold under the impulse of an expressionistic quest. Musically he is paralleled by the great symphonists, Mahler and Shostakovitch, who harken back to the romantic beginning as an overt continuation of that conception. Art is once again explicitly the means of exploring the most profound struggles of existence, especially of life and death. Mahler reaches up through the harrowing neuroses of his own soul toward the transfiguration for which he longs. He knows the dangers of the quest and has shed all of the naïveté of the earlier romantics. This is evident in the extent to which he subjects his own aspirations to sardonic self-mockery. It is painful to overhear his bitter self-doubt but that is also the crucible in which his faith is tried. When the illumination does eventually break through the dark storm clouds, it is received all the more warmly as the grace of bliss. Shostakovitch is a parallel figure, enduring the more prolonged strain of the Stalinist era and without receiving the same transcendent alleviations of his burden. Yet Shostakovitch shows perhaps even more clearly that a human being can still find his way toward the inner dignity that constitutes the whole nobility of existence. All the filth is washed away in that more restrained attainment of serenity.

Naturally, not all twentieth-century artists can measure up to such giants of the human spirit. Many do not engage the most serious questions of existence, its ultimate source and meaning, at all. They immerse themselves in the vividly exciting play of art itself and from their uninhibited inventiveness we get such movements as dada, pop art, performance art, surrealism, and a host of other vastly entertaining episodes. But even within that dizzying profusion of novelties and banalities, the largest talents cannot avoid saying something significant. One thinks of Picasso's concentration on the human figure, especially the female, with its powerful evocation of suffering and destruction. The pathos of the women in Picasso's own life is inescapably exposed, as was the generic suffering of humanity in his most powerful work, *Guernica*. The undoubted power of his technique is confined to the immediate presentation of experience; however, it does not unfold into a deeper meditation on the meaning of the whole. That deeper meditative quest is carried on by a series of artists who have never enjoyed the same public impact. The real successors of the romantics in twentieth-century art are the abstract painters, Malevich, Mondrian, Pollock, and Rothko, who deliberately remove the figurative connection in order to get in touch with the spiritual depth underpinning it all.

The musical equivalent of Picasso is perhaps Stravinsky, a man whose own explorations of the limits of the permissible made him a leading figure of the musical avant-garde. His *Rite of Spring* ballet sent shock waves through the musical world as a powerful return to the most primitive natural impulses. What is curious about Stravinsky is that, like Picasso, he gained an early reputation as a breaker of the molds but his career can best be understood as a search for return to the traditional forms. Just as Picasso rarely strays far from the classical preoccupation with the human figure as his subject, Stravinsky deliberately set out to find the classical musical form that would stabilize the restless spiritual quest of romanticism. He is a leader, with men like Hindemith and Prokofiev, of the return to neoclassical and neobaroque disciplines of music. In their work we begin to see the romantic arc coming full circle. The romantic project is beginning to be rethought from its very inception. Gone is the confidence that we can dispense with the outmoded vessels of meaning that have become opaque and set out on the vast cosmic ocean in search of the meaning whose longing serves as our guide. We are now more conscious of our frailty as single human beings. Accumulated failures, disappointments, and disasters have taken their toll on our initial self-certainty. Now we are more inclined to believe that access to the mystery that surrounds our vulnerable existence can perhaps more securely be found within the traditions that have sustained human life over history. It is an eminently conservative direction in twentieth-century art but not a conservative escape or reaction. Pastiche and imitation are avoided by the conviction that the contemporary evocation of meaning must be within a form that resonates with the world in which we live. It must be a contemporary classical form, not a neoclassical copy.

The extraordinary aspect of this artistic turn is that the search for appropriate forms of meaning, perhaps a more self-conscious concern in music than in the other arts, is not ultimately about forms at all. Form cannot be separated from meaning, and the traditional forms are integrally tied to the meanings they express. The quest for traditional forms, for a contemporary reevocation, cannot be separated from a deeper consideration of the traditional truths they have held. The search for a formal language is inseparable from the search for spiritual meaning. The romantics were mistaken in their conception that the experience of transcendence could be had apart from the revelatory symbols through which it had been expressed. Equally erroneous has been the opposite tendency to assume that the development of artistic language alone, whether articulated as realism, impressionism, cubism, expressionism, surrealism, or whatever, would miraculously yield up the deeper meaning of it all. Language ultimately cannot be separated from the reality it is intended to express, no more than experience can be isolated from either of them. They form a complex of reality-experience-language, and it is those who take the interrelationship seriously who enjoy the best chance of making sense. The romantic beginning that began by dispensing with outmoded tradition now was compelled to return to a deeper examination of those same traditions.

Rediscovery of Tradition

In many respects this is the untold side of the twentieth-century story. We are inclined to regard ourselves as an era precariously set adrift from all steadfast principles and traditions. But the wasteland is not all. While we may lack the spontaneous access to powerfully unreflective truths, that does not mean that we lack the reflective capacity to undertake a deliberate sifting of the remnants of tradition we can recover. This is the hidden side of our time which is full of significance for the future. Although it is little known or appreciated, we live in a period of momentous traditional rediscovery. The fact that it is the work of explicitly historical research, that it seems to be motivated by an admiration for a vanished past, does not mitigate the undoubted appeal and eventually authority that such work of recovery exercises on us. We have a deeper understanding of the ancient and medieval worlds, together with the other great spiritual traditions of mankind, than at any other time in human history. Besides experiencing the scientific explosion, we are also living in the midst of an explosion of historical knowledge. The agnostic Stravinsky has expressed best the deep intuition that guides and sustains the work of historical recovery: "The more one distances oneself from the canons of the Christian Church, the further one distances oneself from the truth. These canons are as true for musical composition as they are for the life of an individual."

What remains is to find the means of making the profound intimations that come to us from the past as well as from our own inner longing transparent for contemporary civilization. That is the challenge that defines the moment in which we live. Within the fragmentation of the modern world we have failed to construct our own meaning, and we are inclined to reexamine more respectfully the fragments of meaning we are left. Can the dried bones be made to live again? The question cannot be answered because it is not yet resolved. All we can do is point to the signs that indicate the direction of the struggle. The most significant such indication is the growing awareness that we cannot dispense even with the fragmentary and opaque elements of the traditions that come down to us. Even great artists are not great enough to construct everything anew and in every generation. They may enlarge and enrich a language, but they must begin with what is given to them, not seek to wholly invent their own. Looking back over the modern period we begin to recognize that even its vaunted assertion of independence from all traditional sources of meaning was an illusion. How could it define itself except in relation to the tradition from which it sought to sever itself? The more we reflect on it, the clearer it becomes that we are not simply unencumbered choosers of traditions, for who we are has already been shaped by the traditions that have more or less chosen us. We do not simply hold onto traditions, they also hold onto us.

Intimations of the revival of traditional forms are, of course, not the same as their revival. We still have a considerable distance to go in the recovery of the symbols whose very opaqueness had been responsible in considerable measure for the lonely odyssey of self-creation that is the modern world. All we have is a new humility before the mysterious depth of traditional meaning. The remark of Stravinsky points toward the truth of Christianity, but it is not yet an embrace of it. This we might characterize as the first stage of the revival process. It begins with respect for the traditional depths viewed from the outside. There is enough of a disposition toward them to move toward utilizing the forms of expression bequeathed by them. It is not yet an entry into the substance of their meaning itself. That is the crucial second stage toward which the formal attractiveness prompts us, prepares us, and even draws us part of the way. The aesthetic can be the first step toward the spiritual reality it embodies. It is in the nature of things that there cannot be an impermeable barrier between the symbol and the symbolized. The whole point of the symbol is indeed to disclose the reality. It is not surprising, therefore, to discover that a movement that begins merely with the aesthetic embrace of traditional spiritual forms ends up realizing an existential participation in them as well.

The continuum between beauty and truth is, as the philosophers knew, seamless. To interpose an obstacle between them introduces a note of inauthenticity that threatens the integrity of the artistic enterprise. We cannot acknowledge the aesthetic truth of the spiritual movement without acknowledging its authoritative force in our own lives. Further, we are required to place ourselves under the guidance of the traditional sources of the meaning that discloses itself to us. That is the decisive turning point. It is no longer for us to make the traditions live again; rather, it is to allow them to work their enlivening effect within our lives. The resonances that still come to us, the intimations that disclose the transcendent mystery guarding our existence, can scarcely be known apart from the remnants of tradition still present within us. We realize that the exploration of mystery, far from being possible by dint of our own creative efforts, would not even have a beginning without the fragmentary presence of traditional forms. It is not that the traditional sources of meaning have died so much as we have failed to awaken to them. Despite all its best efforts the modern world that sought to live outside of traditions now discovers that it has never really escaped their embrace. Without traditional forms there would simply be no meaning.

One of the risks of the artistic life is that it can lead to just such a deepening of the life of the artist. Accounts of religious conversion are in fact common among twentieth-century writers and artists. But it is the musicians who most dramatically embody the shift because their work directly serves the spiritual cult itself. One of the astonishing recent developments has been the enormous popularity and success of explicitly liturgical works performed in the concert hall. This does not mean that they could not be performed in churches, but indicates that they have found a wider transparence that renders them accessible even in the nonliturgical setting. The pioneer of this kind of music is undoubtedly Olivier Messiaen, whose output is largely centered on a meditative unfolding of Catholic mystical theology. But more recently a new generation of composers led by Arvo Pärt, Henryk Gorecki, John Tavener, and others have exploded on the public scene with works that are grounded in the musical traditions of their respective faiths. This is music that is different from the preceding exploration of the established musical forms. It is not a mere borrowing of spiritual elements in the service of music. This is the real thing. Whatever the final judgment of artistic merits, there can be no doubt that this is music that is seriously and unreservedly in the service of spiritual meaning.

That, it turns out, is the secret of its appeal. A work of such unprepossessing character as Pärt's *Passion of Our Lord According to St. John* derives most of its effect from the unwavering faith with which it is sung. The music itself is minimal, consisting only of variations on short sung phrases, thus virtually requiring the weight to be placed on the spiritual meaning itself. Something similar is the case with Gorecki's enormously popular *Third Symphony*, subtitled a *Symphony of Sorrowful Songs*. The long first movement consists of a disarmingly simple canon that is nevertheless varied profoundly to maintain our interest in the long meditative arc it unfolds. That leads us into the sorrowful songs themselves, which include a prayer scribbled on a Gestapo prison cell wall, a lamentation of Mary at the foot of the Cross, and a traditional Polish song about the loss of a child. It is music that probes the limit of human suffering but without a hint of protest at the injustice of the fate endured. What makes it a work of powerful spirituality is that the suffering, which is real, has been utterly transfigured through its redemptive surrender to God. It is faith in the divine mystery beyond it all that renders what would otherwise be a mere complaint into a work of transcendent serenity. Its resonance goes directly to the human heart.

As with a work like Tavener's *Protecting Veil*, which powerfully evokes the protection of Mary by means of a cello voice and a string orchestra, it is difficult not to conclude that something new is in evidence here. The supposedly opaque traditions, previously perceived as the major obstacle to the transparence of meaning, now turn out to possess a depth beyond our imagination. By yielding to their promptings, by entering into the order they constitute, they disclose their riches to us. What could be no more than an object of admiration when viewed from the outside turns out to contain the fullness of reality once we yield to its existential force. By thinking we could make the elements of traditions serve our construction of meaning we had lost the only meaning available to us. But now the great discovery has been made that the opening of publicly authoritative meaning is possible once we submit to its ordering influence in our lives.

The modern conceit had been that we could find our own way back to the illuminative center of meaning. We already possessed sufficient light of our own to reveal the path before us. The outmoded remnants of traditions could safely be discarded in the face of this limitless self-confidence. But then we discovered that without a point of reference in the givenness of the world that we could not even take the first steps anywhere. Having become independent of all received sources of meaning we now were blown about without either an anchor or a compass to fix our position. We had peeled away the last layer of the onion only to discover our hands were empty. The illusion that we could from a superior vantage point critique all positions had proved a cruel self-deception. Thinking we could see through all things we ended by no longer having anything to see. Now we discover that we are creatures of time and space in which the limits of our vision is what has historically been transmitted to us. There is no going back to a beginning before the beginning nor forward to an end that is outside of the whole. Even the effort to attune our existence in relation to transcendent Being cannot dispense with the recognition that revelation occurs within a historically unfolded tradition.

This is what makes the artistic exploration of meaning the most open medium of inquiry. It is tied to the concrete experience of reality, moving outward from the dimensions that immediately impinge upon us. Almost by its very nature art responds to the concretely symbolic pulls that tug upon us. This is why even for professed atheists art still resonates with transcendent mystery. Something similar occurs in the concrete struggle to build social and political meaning. It is a matter of indifference where we begin so long as we do begin. By entering on the first steps the dynamic of disclosure takes over and expanses of meaning are discovered that at the beginning were barely suspected. But in each case we must entrust ourselves to the remnants of meaning that remain. We cannot begin with the Cartesian elimination of all traditional sources because we will then only be left locked within the loneliness of the ego. That has been the cruel illusion from which the modern world is only now beginning to recover.

We recognize that our existence is guarded by the mystery of transcendent Being which is the source of all vitality and meaning. And we have overcome the illusion that the miraculous horizon could be reached through our own efforts. Instead, we must place ourselves under its revelatory promptings, recognizing that this is the way of all human history and finding within the unsuspected depths of tradition the resources we so sorely lacked within ourselves. In this way the transcendent source of meaning is restored to modern civilization in a fully self-conscious way. Our errors have taught us that the transcendent horizon cannot be constructed through our own paltry efforts nor can it be reduced to some mundane dimension of our social or political world. It is what guards the meaning of existence precisely because it transcends all existence. We cannot penetrate beyond that mystery, nor can we dispense with the halting historical process by which the mystery reveals itself to us. Only the traditions, albeit in fragmentary form, contain the true resonance of transcendent revelation. There is no other knowledge outside of them. By taking up the invitation they gently extend to us we begin to discover the only route toward transcendent illumination that is possible for human beings. We accept the status we have been assigned in the order of the whole. Not being gods, we can acknowledge God and receive from him the gift of participation in the divine life. Once freed from the impossible burden of providing our own meaning to ourselves, we can accept the surpassing divine outpouring of reality. By accepting the gift of transcendent life as our goal we have at the same time received the gift of meaning within this life.

BIBLIOGRAPHIC NOTE

As is evident, this book is more in the mode of a meditation than in that of a scholarly treatise. Its principal intent is to follow out the lines of reflection that discernably emerge from the chaos of our world. Scholarship is undoubtedly one of the tools that serve that purpose, but it is not the primary mode by which the transparence of existence can be apprehended and communicated. Indeed, one of the implications of the preceding essay is that scholarship itself rests on a set of presuppositions that are far from self-subsistent. We tend to overlook the contextual dependence of the world of learning precisely because it is a world constituted by a common set of assumptions. This is of course why the different fields of knowledge often find one another incomprehensible: they may not share the same starting points. There is a need therefore for scholars to periodically step back from their disciplines, in order to attempt a freestanding formulation of their insights for the edification of that most elusive of all prey, the well-disposed general reader. Such has been my goal.

Having now completed the effort, fairness also obliges me and the interest of readers compels me to include something by way of recognition of the scholarly debts that underlie it. A meditation may stand or fall on its own merits, but no one arrives at its elaboration without the illumination extended by a great many others. Curious readers too will naturally want to know what an author has read, both from a general interest in understanding the arguments better and a more specific interest in pursuing it further on their own. Accordingly, I am happy to append this bibliographic note by which the sympathetic might be further guided and the suspicious more fully confirmed. I make no claim to the originality of the reflections I have pursued, not only because of the manifest limits of my own abilities, but more essentially because originality is not a particularly prized value in the search for truth. What matters is not from whence an idea comes but whither it leads us. Does it bring us a step closer to a fuller appreciation of the reality in which we find ourselves? Toward a more adequate attunement to the order of Being? At the end of the day truth stands in judgment over authority, and whatever merit the latter possesses is entirely derivative from that subordination. Like the scribe of the New Testament, we are charged with searching through treasures old and new in order to bring forth what is of value (Mt 13:52).

Among such contemporary treasures in the meditative recovery of meaning, few figure more prominently than Eric Voegelin. As a member of the European emigré constellation who arrived in America as a result of the Nazi upheaval, Voegelin, together with Hannah Arendt, Leo Strauss, and others, brought about a rediscovery of the greatness of classical political philosophy as well as renewed respect for the revealed traditions. Voegelin stands out from their broader efforts at the recovery of premodern sources of wisdom by virtue of his penetration of the experiential roots. His is a unique enterprise that finds its closest parallel among the novelists and artists who put us directly in touch with the sources of ideas in life itself. His great work, *Order and History* in five volumes, *Israel and Revelation, The World of the Polis, Plato and Aristotle, The Ecumenic Age,* and *In Search of Order* (Louisiana State University Press, 1956–1985), provides the most perceptive account of the experiential movements by which the ordering symbols of human history have emerged. Together with the other volumes of his *Collected Works* (all in publication from the University of Missouri Press) it is by far the best education in the meditative and revelatory dynamics from which all meaning arises. Other more recent approaches to the same problematic of the prearticulate sources of order within human experience include Charles Taylor, *Sources of the Self* (Harvard University Press, 1989) and a more popular version in *The Ethics of Authenticity* (Harvard University Press, 1992).

The much larger literature on the crisis of meaning in the modern era includes particularly Leo Strauss's *Natural Right and History* (University of Chicago Press, 1953), Hannah Arendt's *Origins of Totalitarianism* (Vintage, 1968), Henri de Lubac's *Drama of Atheist Humanism* (New American Library, 1950), and Albert Camus's *The Rebel* (Vintage, 1956), as well as Voegelin's *New Science of Politics* (University of Chicago Press, 1952). They are all in one way or another classic midcentury statements concerning the bankruptcy of modernity in light of the totalitarian convulsion, and they are completed by the final demolition of communist legitimacy accomplished by Alexander Solzhenitsyn's *Gulag Archipelago* (3 vols.; 1974–1978).

Since then we have a more pervasive body of writing that exemplifies as much as it observes the collapse of all possible sources of meaning in the contemporary world. It is a mode of reflection perhaps best represented by Jacques Derrida in such works as *Of Grammatology* (Johns Hopkins University Press, 1974), by Michel Foucault in *The Order of Things* (Vintage, 1973), and—with a more American flavor—by Richard Rorty in *Contingency, Irony, and Solidarity* (Cambridge University Press, 1989). I have sought to avoid emphasizing the obviously "deconstructionist" tenor of their reflections, in order to draw attention to the deeper quest for construction by which alone interest in the project of deconstruction can be sustained. Among the more interesting exemplars of a thoroughly contemporary mode of reflection that goes beyond such self-imposed inhibitions I would mention Václav Havel, especially essays like "The Power of the Powerless" in *Open Letters: Selected Writings 1965–1990* (Vintage, 1992) and *Letters to Olga* (Knopf, 1988). My own examination of such matters are contained in *After Ideology: Recovering the Spiritual Foundations of Freedom* (The Catholic University of America Press, 1995).

Any attempt to grapple adequately with the crisis of meaning that has spawned the postmodern age must reach out toward the great thinkers of the modern era who struggled mightily with its ramifications. For this reason my text is sprinkled with references to Nietzsche, especially his *Will to Power* (Vintage, 1967) and *Thus Spoke Zarathustra* (Penguin, 1967). Equally we must refer to the only figure from whom Nietzsche admitted he had anything to learn, Fyodor Dostoevsky, whose searing exploration of the crisis of faith at the heart of the modern world is unrivaled. In contrast to Nietzsche, however, Dostoevsky sought to find his way back to Christ, most especially in the portrayal of "The Legend of the Grand Inquisitor" within *The Brothers Karamazov*. A parallel exploration is conducted slightly earlier by Søren Kierkegaard, any of whose works yield fruitful insight into what it means to communicate faith in a faithless world. In a still unrecognized way, Martin Heidegger is a curious heir to these great nineteenth-century explorers. It comes out best in his two volumes simply called *Nietzsche* (HarperSanFrancisco, 1979–1984). I am presently at work on a larger study of such pioneers whose struggles are capable of yielding a fuller account of the transparence of the modern world.

The whole impact of this deepest reconsideration of the modern world is to send us further back to the great and classic sources. We are directed to a rereading of classical philosophy, particularly Plato and Aristotle, in recognition that the philosophical mode of reflection is entirely their discovery and finds its preeminent expression in their hands. Equally, we are driven deeper into the word of revelation, the Scriptures that have been handed down, as well as the historical turning points of their absorption. Saint Augustine and Saint Thomas are surely such moments when all of the strands of the Western tradition, Greek, Roman, Jewish, Islamic, and Christian, are brought into conversation. Today we are at such a point of mutual engagement of the great spiritual traditions that now definitively includes the non-Western experiences. It is no accident that the most perceptive voices of the day are supremely conscious of the global reach of the conversation. Among such mediators I would certainly number Pope John Paul II, whose intellectual range is most fully evident in his last three encyclicals, *Veritatis Splendor*, *Evangelium Vitae*, and *Fides et Ratio*.

Having drunk deeply of the great spiritual traditions and their philosophical expositions, we cannot overlook the necessity of authoritative political forms for our world. The liberal consensual language of individual rights may be at the core of such constructions but their implementation requires a fuller explication of the sources and significance. A reconsideration of the liberal political tradition is an integral component of the broader reconsideration of the modern world. The classic liberal sources include among others the works of John Locke, Alexis de Tocqueville, and John Stuart Mill, as well as the American Framers. In the contemporary setting the conversation is carried on most interestingly by the transition from John Rawls's *Theory of Justice* (Harvard University Press, 1971) to his more recent *Political Liberalism* (Columbia University Press, 1993). Those who are interested in my more extended study of such matters may consult *The Growth of the Liberal Soul* (University of Missouri Press, 1997).

Whether the search for meaning follows the narrower parameters of political order or ranges through the depths of metaphysics, an irreducible dimension is constituted by the unmediated experiences of art. Some of the discussion in the text is derived from the particular strand of modern painting delineated by Robert Rosenblum, *Modern Painting and the Northern Romantic Tradition: Friedrich to Rothko* (Thames and Hudson, 1975). On the spiritual in modern art, see Roger Lipsey, *An Art of Our Own: The Spiritual in Twentieth Century Art* (Shambala, 1988). For an approach to literary texts with wider implications for the philosophy of art, the work of Mikhail Bakhtin is to be highly recommended. Among writers, Walker Percy is surely of particular interest, not least of all for his short book of hilarious quirky meditations entitled *Lost in the Cosmos* (Washington Square, 1984). It is only one of the many instances of a genre I have had before me as an unattainable model for my own efforts. Short direct books that contain more than their simplicity belies include not only G. K. Chesterton's *Orthodoxy* but also C. S. Lewis's *Abolition of Man* and E. F. Schumacher's *Guide for the Perplexed*, to name but the most obvious candidates. Together with the preceding suggestions for further reading they constitute the royal road toward a wisdom to which I can only point.